Product huMan

Product huMan

Seeing Life Through the Lens of Product Management. One Feature at a Time

Rupa Bhagwat

Rupa Bhagwat
Product huMan
Seeing Life Through the Lens of Product Management. One Feature at a Time

Cover design: Rupa Bhagwat
Interior design: Rupa Bhagwat
Image Credits: Images by Rupa Bhagwat
Printed in the United States of America [2025]

All rights reserved
Copyright © 2025 by Rupa Bhagwat

No part of this publication may be reproduced, distributed, or transmitted in any form or by any means, including photocopying, recording, or other electronic or mechanical methods, without the prior written permission of the publisher, except in the case of brief quotations embodied in critical reviews and certain other noncommercial uses permitted by copyright law.

Disclaimer
All characters, events, and entities portrayed in this book are purely fictional. Any resemblance to real persons, living or dead, or actual events is entirely coincidental. The names, places, and incidents are the product of the author's imagination and are not intended to reflect any real-world individuals, organizations, or locations.

Published by Spines Publishing Platform
ISBN: 979-8-89691-045-9

Dedication

In this heartfelt dedication, I express my deepest gratitude to those who have shaped my journey and inspired me to write this book. First and foremost, I am forever indebted to my parents, whose unwavering support and encouragement have been the bedrock of my life. They have always believed in my uniqueness and ability to achieve anything I set my mind to. Papa, in particular, has been a constant source of inspiration, affectionately referring to me as a Vimaan(an airplane), a metaphor for his unwavering belief that I was born to shine and soar high in the sky. Happy retirement, Papa! This is a small gift from me to your healthy and enjoyable retirement journey! Thank you, Mumma, for teaching me the importance of consistency, dedication, and sacrifice.

I extend my heartfelt thanks to Pooja, my well-wisher, guide, teacher, best friend, and godmother. Your constant trust in me has been a beacon of light, even in my darkest hours. You have always made me feel like the strongest person in the world, capable of weathering any storm that comes my way. Your pride in me has never faltered, and your willingness to answer my calls at 3 a.m. has been a testament to your dedication, love, and tremendous care.

Last, but certainly not least, my heartfelt gratitude goes to my incredible siblings, Pradnya and Shubham. You both have been my greatest inspiration. The lessons I've learned from you surpass anything I could have gained elsewhere. Thank you for pushing me to become the strongest version of myself.

Contents

Preface

Life is a journey full of twists and turns, challenges, aspirations, and relationships, and just like all of you, I've had my share of navigating through it. I've come to realize that the most powerful and transformative journey is one where we view ourselves as products. This idea, which has shaped much of my professional life, is something I now bring into every aspect of my personal journey. What if the same principles that make great products—thoughtful design, continuous improvement, and intentional decisions—could also help us live more fulfilling lives?

This idea didn't just come out of nowhere. It grew from my own experiences, both personal and professional. As a product manager, I've spent over a decade making decisions in uncertain environments, learning from both successes and failures. At one point, while going through a rough patch in my life, it struck me how much product management and life have in common. Both require us to make tough decisions, adapt to changing circumstances, and constantly work toward being a better version of ourselves. That realization became my guiding philosophy: to apply the structured thinking of product management to my life and, in doing so, create a sense of clarity and purpose amidst the chaos.

It dawned on me that product management is, at its core, about making choices and steering toward the best possible path amidst uncertainty. Life, in many ways, mirrors this process. While we may not have the power to meticulously design life's trajectory, we can certainly craft the blueprint of a product with intention and purpose. So, I thought, why not intertwine the principles of product management with the framework of life? This realization became my guiding philosophy: applying the structured methodologies of product management to bring clarity and direction to my personal journey.

This book is not just a culmination of my professional experiences but a reflection of my countless personal adventures and challenges. For over a decade, I've traversed the landscape of product management, learning from every triumph and setback and gathering wisdom from those who have generously shared their knowledge. These experiences, coupled with the invaluable conversations I've had during several networking events—where I invited others to imagine their lives as products—have profoundly influenced the content of this book.

Why am I writing this book? Because I believe this approach can help others too. In today's fast-paced, hyper-connected world, where social media often takes precedence over real human connections, it's easy to lose touch with our personal lives and emotional well-being.

We are all products—the greatest products of all—**humankind**! Through these pages, I aim to impart the foundational knowledge of product management, not just as a professional skill but as a life skill. By understanding these principles, you will learn how to apply them to simplify your life, improve your relationships, and find your true purpose.

This book is my attempt to bridge the gap between professional skills and personal growth. It's not just about product management as a career; it's about using these principles to simplify your life, strengthen your relationships, and find your true purpose. It's about helping you reconnect with yourself and the people around you.

Through these pages, I hope to show you how to manage the "products" in your life—your relationships, career, and personal growth—with the same care and intentionality that go into building great products. We'll explore how to identify your goals, measure success, and build a "team" of supportive people around you. We'll even examine the users in your life—from early adopters to latecomers—and how to navigate these dynamics with grace and understanding.

Ultimately, this book is an invitation to see yourself as a constantly evolving product—one that adapts, grows, and improves with time. My hope is that by the end of this journey, you'll feel more in control of your life, more connected to your purpose, and more equipped to handle whatever comes your way.

This isn't just my story; it's a collective journey inspired by all the people who've shared their stories, ideas, and insights with me over the years. I'm deeply grateful to everyone who has walked this path with me, and I hope that together, we can take steps toward making life—not just for ourselves, but for everyone—a little better, one feature at a time.

With heartfelt thanks,

Rupa

Introduction

Picture yourself at a bustling farmers market, where every vendor is eagerly showcasing their goods, each offering something uniquely their own. The air is alive with the rich scents of fresh fruits, baked goods, spices, and perfumes, mingling with the sounds of lively negotiations. As you wander through this vibrant scene, you're not just a buyer; you're a participant—a product that's been carefully crafted, presented, and assessed by those around you. Think of yourself as that quirky artisanal jam stand—offbeat, unique, and definitely not for everyone, but those who get you, really get you.

Every interaction, every relationship, every decision you make is part of this grand market where the currency isn't just money but trust, respect, and value. However, unlike the farmers market, in this marketplace of life, you're both a product and a product manager. Navigating this world is more than physical placement or image; it means making choices that align with your values, honing your skills, and positioning yourself for success. But how do you ensure you're not just surviving but thriving in such a complex environment? It's not like we can all hire a personal life coach to shout motivational quotes at us every morning, right?

The key lies in applying the principles of product management to your personal life.

Product management isn't just a business discipline; it's a way of thinking that can revolutionize how you approach life itself. By grasping the fundamentals of product management—ranging from behavioral economics to narrative design—you can craft a life that's not only fulfilling but also aligned with your deepest values and goals. And through this book, I invite you to view your life through the lens of product management, by guiding you to become the most successful, resilient, and authentic version of yourself.

The reality is that the intersection of professional and personal growth is often overlooked. Too often, we compartmentalize our lives, treating our careers and personal lives as separate entities. Yet, the skills and strategies that make us successful professionally can also enhance our personal lives. Take, for example, product management principles—they're tools that can simplify our lives, help us set clear goals, and guide us toward continuous improvement. This book aims to bridge that gap, taking what we learn in our careers and applying it to our personal lives to create a cohesive and fulfilling existence.

In today's fast-paced world, the ability to manage oneself effectively is becoming increasingly crucial. Just as businesses need to adapt to changing market conditions, individuals need to adapt to the complexities of modern life. These pages will equip you with the tools to do just that, by teaching you how to apply product management principles to both your personal and professional development.

This information is for anyone navigating life, careers, and relationships. Whether you're a young professional just starting out, someone midway through your career looking to make meaningful changes, or someone seeking to deepen your relationships, these concepts can help. To get the most out of this book, approach it with an open mind and a willingness to apply the principles discussed. Reflect on your life as you read and consider how each concept can be tailored to your unique circumstances.

To maximize the benefits of this book, engage actively with the exercises and reflections provided in each chapter. These are designed to help you internalize and apply the concepts to your own life. Take time to journal your thoughts, set specific goals, and track your progress as you move through the book. Remember, the goal isn't just to learn new ideas but to implement them in a way that brings tangible improvements to your life.

Chapter 1
The Basics of Product Management Applied to Life

At its core, product management is about discovering, creating and capturing value. It's the art and science of transforming an idea into something that meets the needs of its target audience. A product manager's job is to guide this process from the initial concept through development, launch, and beyond, ensuring that the product remains relevant and valuable over time. This process requires a deep understanding of the market, the users, and the product's unique value proposition. But product management isn't just a professional skill; it's a mindset that can be applied to every aspect of life. And when I say this, I mean the smallest part of your life can be strategized well by using product management tools and techniques. Imagine you want to optimize your Netflix binge-watching, product management can help you do that- because let's be honest, that's important too.

Each of us is a product, continually evolving, adapting, and striving to meet the needs of the world around us. Just as a product manager must understand the market and user's needs, you must understand yourself and the people around you. You're both the product and the product manager, responsible for shaping your development, making decisions about what aspects of yourself to prioritize, and positioning yourself in a way that aligns with your goals.

As we navigate through life, it's important to recognize that our decisions are often influenced by more than just logic. Behavioral economics and psychology shed light on the cognitive biases and heuristics that guide our decision-making processes. For instance, **confirmation bias**—our tendency to favor information that confirms our existing beliefs—can impact everything from our career choices to our personal relationships. It is the tendency to favor information that supports what we already believe—shows up everywhere. Like when you justify eating cake for breakfast because, hey, it has eggs, so it's basically breakfast food, right? Similarly, **loss aversion**, where the fear of losing something outweighs the potential gains, can prevent us from taking necessary risks that could lead to personal growth.

Understanding these biases can help you become more mindful of how you approach decisions, ensuring that your choices align with your true values rather than being unconsciously influenced by these psychological factors.

Now, this idea of being a product might seem like a new concept, but it's actually grounded in well-established product management principles developed over decades. That's why it's important to gain some context on the product life cycle.

The Concept of the Product Life Cycle in Personal Growth

The discipline of product management has come a long way over the decades. It started in the manufacturing industry, focusing mainly on the production and distribution of physical goods. But as technology advanced and markets became more complex, product management expanded to include software, services, and even digital experiences. Today's product managers navigate intricate ecosystems, understand user psychology, and leverage data to make informed decisions. This evolution mirrors the complexities we face in our personal lives, where we must adapt to changing circumstances, embrace new technologies, and continuously refine our approach to personal growth.

Just like a product, our lives follow a lifecycle—introduction, growth, maturity, and eventually, decline. By viewing your life as a product, you can approach each stage with a clear strategy. Focus on growth during the early stages of your career, maintain and refine your skills as you reach maturity, and when necessary, reinvent yourself to avoid decline. This analogy encourages you to regularly assess where you are in life and make proactive decisions to ensure ongoing growth and fulfilment.

Let's break down each stage of the product lifecycle with real-life examples to see how it applies to your personal journey:

- **The Introduction Phase:** At this phase, the product —or in this case, you—are new to the market. This is like the first day at a new job where you're trying to remember everyone's names, hoping you don't accidentally microwave fish in the break room. You're in the early stages of your career or personal development and there is no room for the social mishap, which might create a barrier between you and your career goals. For instance, picking up a fight with your boss during initial days of your career is not a good idea. Additionally, you might be learning new skills, building your network, or exploring different career paths. Just like a product's planning, your focus should be on establishing yourself, gaining visibility, and building your brand.

Some examples of the introductory phase are early career focus or finding a life partner or starting a new college degree, where you have to choose a stream that is in alignment with your goals. If you've just landed your first job out of college, this is your introduction phase. Your primary goals are learning the ropes, understanding your strengths, and positioning yourself for future opportunities. Much like a product gaining initial traction, your success at this stage will depend on your ability to adapt, learn quickly, and make a positive impression on those around you.

- **The Growth Phase:** During the growth phase, the product starts to gain traction, and the focus shifts to expanding market share. In your life, this phase might correspond to advancing in your career, taking on more responsibilities, or deepening your personal relationships. It's a time of rapid development and opportunity, but it also comes with challenges like increased pressure and the need to continuously prove yourself.

Climbing the career ladder illustrates the growth phase. Imagine you've been in your industry for a few years, and you're starting to climb the ranks. You're taking on leadership roles, managing larger projects, or even considering starting your own business. Just as a growing product must innovate to stay competitive, you must continue developing your skills, expanding your network, and seeking new challenges to sustain your growth.

- **The Maturity Phase:** The maturity phase is when the product is well-established and enjoys a stable position in the market. In your personal life, this might be when you've reached a comfortable level of success—perhaps you're in a senior role, have built a strong network, or have achieved a balanced work-life integration. However, maturity can also bring complacency, so it's important to continue innovating and finding new ways to add value.

Sustaining success is a prime example of the maturity phase. If you've reached a senior position in your company, the challenge becomes maintaining your success and avoiding stagnation. Which, let's face it, is the corporate equivalent of avoiding that extra slice of pizza you know you don't need—but will probably eat anyway. Like a mature product that must differentiate itself to prevent decline, you need to stay relevant by mentoring others, exploring new interests, or even reinventing your career.

- **The Decline and Reinvention Phase:** Eventually, every product faces decline unless it reinvents itself.

> This stage could represent a time in your life when you feel stuck, unchallenged, or ready for a change. It might be time to pivot—whether that's starting a new career, learning a new skill, or pursuing a different passion. Reinvention is crucial to avoid the natural decline that comes from staying in the same place for too long.

An excellent example of the decline and reinvention phase is the career pivot. Suppose you've been in the same industry for decades, and you feel your passion is waning. Rather than letting yourself slip into decline, you might decide to pivot—perhaps by starting a consultancy, exploring a new field, or going back to school. Just as products must innovate to survive, you need to be willing to make bold changes to keep your life dynamic and fulfilling.

With an understanding of these product phases, you can begin to see where habits and decision-making in life are similar to product management.

Neuroscience and Product Management

A lot of people ask me about how Neuroscience is connected with Product Development, well Neuroscience plays a very important role in product development by offering insights into how users perceive, interact with, and make decisions about products. Understanding the brain's mechanisms, such as attention, memory, and emotion, allows product teams to design experiences that align with users' cognitive and emotional needs. For instance, leveraging concepts like dopamine-driven reward systems can enhance user engagement, while insights into cognitive load help streamline interfaces for ease of use. Neuroscience also sheds light on biases like loss aversion and decision fatigue, enabling the creation of features that reduce friction and build trust. By integrating these principles, product developers can craft solutions that not only meet functional requirements but also resonate deeply with users on a psychological level, driving adoption and satisfaction.

Neuroscience provides valuable insights into how our brains influence our habits and decisions. Habits are deeply ingrained behaviors that free up cognitive resources, allowing us to focus on more complex tasks. However, creating new habits—or breaking old ones—requires understanding the **cue-routine-reward** loop that governs habit formation. By identifying the triggers (cues) that lead to certain behaviors (routines) and the rewards that reinforce them, you can design strategies to build better habits.

Additionally, our decision-making is often influenced by the state of our **prefrontal cortex**, the part of the brain responsible for reasoning and impulse control. When stressed or fatigued, our ability to make sound decisions diminishes. This explains why you once decided that 3 AM was the perfect time to start a home workout routine... only to regret it the next morning. Which is why managing stress and maintaining mental clarity is crucial for effective decision-making.

By understanding the neuroscience behind habits and decisions, you can design a life cycle (product cycle) that aligns with your goals, fostering routines that support your long-term success. Doing so requires incorporating more advanced principles.

Advanced Product Management Principles in Personal Life

Now that you've got the basics down, it's time to dive into more advanced principles. These concepts not only enhance the value you create but also help you navigate the complexities of life with greater clarity and purpose.

Behavioral Data Analytics: Tracking Personal Progress

In product management, data analytics is key for understanding user behavior, predicting outcomes, and making informed decisions. Similarly, in your personal life, tracking your behaviors, habits, and outcomes can provide invaluable insights into your growth and areas that need improvement. Key Performance Indicators (KPIs) play a central role in measuring success, synthesizing data insights, and driving actionable decisions. For instance, when launching a fitness app, a product manager might track KPIs like daily active users, retention rates, or average session duration. These metrics help refine the user experience, ensuring the app aligns with user needs and drives engagement.

Similarly, in your personal life, setting KPIs for your habits and goals can be transformative. Tracking behaviors like daily exercise duration, hours of focused work, or quality sleep allows you to analyze patterns and optimize for better outcomes. Journaling, for example, is a practical tool for behavioral data analytics—recording your thoughts, habits, and progress provides data points to measure growth and identify areas needing adjustment.

If you notice through your personal analytics that you're

more productive after morning exercise, you can align your routine accordingly, much like how a product manager adjusts features to boost user satisfaction. Ignoring these personal KPIs, akin to disregarding critical product metrics, can lead to inefficiencies or even burnout. Just as refining a product based on user data ensures its success, periodically reviewing and acting on your own life data ensures continuous growth and well-being.

A practical way to apply behavioral data analytics in your life is through journaling. By regularly recording your thoughts, experiences, and progress, you can identify patterns in your behavior and emotions. For example, you might notice that you're more productive when you exercise in the morning or that certain activities increase your stress levels. This data allows you to tweak your routine, optimize your time, and enhance your overall well-being.

One common mistake is ignoring the data you collect about yourself. Just as a product manager must analyze user data to refine a product, you need to pay attention to the signals your body and mind are sending you. Ignoring signs of burnout, stress, or dissatisfaction can lead to long-term consequences. So, it's crucial to regularly review your personal analytics and make the necessary changes to your habits and lifestyle.

Reflection and Actionable Advice:

- Start journaling or using a habit-tracking app to monitor your daily activities and emotions.
- Set aside time each week to review your entries, looking for patterns and areas where you can improve.

- Use this data to make informed decisions about your routines, relationships, and personal goals.

Gamification: An Introduction

For now, know that gamification is a powerful tool in product management, often used to boost user engagement and motivation by introducing game-like elements into non-game contexts. We will get into more details in a later chapter. However, keep this concept in mind because you can apply this principle to your personal development, making the process of self-improvement more enjoyable and rewarding.

Consider turning your personal goals into a game by setting up a point system or reward structure. Finally, a chance to turn your life into a video game—minus the dramatic boss battles, of course. Unless you count dealing with your boss as one. For instance, you could award yourself points for completing daily tasks like exercising, reading, or practicing a new skill. Once you accumulate a certain number of points, you could reward yourself with something you enjoy, like a special treat or a day off. This approach not only makes goal setting more fun but also helps you stay motivated and track your progress.

A word of caution: a common pitfall with gamification is making the system too complex or rigid, which can lead to frustration or burnout. The key is to keep it simple and flexible because if your life starts resembling a spreadsheet of a thousand data points, it's probably time to reassess your approach. Your goal is to boost motivation, not create additional stress. If you find the system becoming a burden, simplify it or take a break.

Reflection and Actionable Advice:

- Choose one or two areas of your life where you want to apply gamification, such as fitness or learning a new skill.
- Create a simple point system or reward structure that encourages consistent progress.
- Regularly assess how the gamification process is working for you and adjust it as needed to ensure it remains enjoyable and effective.

So far, it might seem like applying product management principles to life isn't as complicated as you thought. If that's the case, great! But here's where the fun really begins. The advanced concepts are more internal and personal. You'll also need to consider that different aspects of your life require different approaches, just like how products vary depending on their target market or delivery method.

Let's dive into that next!

Types of "Products" You Encounter in Life

In product management, products are often categorized based on their target market or delivery method. This same idea can be applied to different aspects of your life, helping you understand how to manage and optimize your personal and professional relationships. Let's explore the various product categories and how they translate:

- **B2B (Business-to-Business) Relationships:** In business, B2B relationships involve transactions between companies, where one business provides products or services to another. These relationships are inherently deeper and more intricate because they often require significant trust, collaboration, and mutual understanding to succeed. In your personal life, B2B relationships are akin to your professional connections—your network of colleagues, mentors, and industry peers. This is like a B2B partnership—both sides invest time and effort to create value. Managing these relationships requires a clear understanding of mutual goals and a commitment to nurturing connections that can help you grow in your career.

Mentorship is a perfect example of a B2B relationship. Think of the relationship between you and a mentor. This is a B2B relationship where you, as the mentee, benefit from the mentor's knowledge and experience. In return, the mentor gains the satisfaction of helping you grow and the fresh perspective you bring to their work. To manage this relationship effectively, you need to be clear about what you want to learn and how you can contribute to the relationship. This might involve setting clear goals for your mentorship, being proactive in seeking feedback, and finding ways to add value to your mentor's life—like offering to help with projects or sharing insights from your own experiences.

- **B2C (Business-to-Consumer) Relationships:** B2C relationships in business are more transactional, with a focus on satisfying the immediate needs of individual consumers. These relationships rely heavily on the emotional connection between the consumer and the brand. In your personal life, these are your relationships with friends, family, and loved ones. These relationships are more emotional and less transactional, but they still require careful management. Just as a consumer chooses a product based on its ability to meet their needs, the people in your life are drawn to you based on the qualities and values you bring to the table.

Think about your relationship with a close friend. While not transactional in the traditional sense, this relationship is based on a mutual exchange of emotional support, trust, and companionship. To maintain this relationship, you need to be attentive to your friend's needs, just as a business must be responsive to its customers. This could involve being a good listener, offering support during tough times, or simply spending quality time together. By understanding and meeting the emotional needs of your loved ones, you can build stronger, more fulfilling relationships.

- **SaaS (Software as a Service) in Personal Routines:** SaaS products are designed to provide ongoing value through a subscription-based model, continually evolving to meet user needs. In your personal life, SaaS can be compared to the routines and habits you build to support your well-being. These daily practices—like exercise, meditation, or time management strategies—help you function effectively. Just as SaaS products require regular updates and improvements, your routines need to be adaptable and responsive to changes in your life.

Consider your morning routine. Maybe you start your day with a workout, followed by a healthy breakfast and some time to review your goals for the day. Much like a SaaS product, this routine is designed to provide ongoing value by setting you up for success. However, as your life changes—maybe you start a new job or your family grows—you might need to tweak your routine to ensure it continues to meet your needs. For instance, you might need to wake up earlier to fit in your workout or find a new way to prioritize your goals. Regularly assessing and adjusting your routines can ensure they continue to serve you well.

- **IVR (Interactive Voice Response) in Communication Styles:** IVR systems guide users through a series of options, helping them find the information or assistance they need. Similarly, your communication style is how you interact with others, guiding them through conversations and relationships. Effective communication is about being responsive, clear, and empathetic—qualities essential for personal and professional success.

Think back to the last difficult conversation you had with a colleague or loved one. How did you handle it? Did you listen carefully to the other person's concerns? Did you respond in a way that was clear and respectful? Your ability to communicate effectively is like an IVR system, guiding the interaction toward a positive outcome. For instance, in a conflict situation, effective communication might involve acknowledging the other person's feelings, clearly expressing your needs, and working together to find a solution that satisfies both parties. By honing your communication skills, you can build stronger, more positive relationships.

Each product type offers a unique perspective on managing different aspects of your life. By understanding these analogies, you can begin to see how product management principles apply to your relationships, routines, and communication strategies. In the next chapter, we'll dive into identifying your core values and building the foundation for your personal product.

Chapter 2
Identifying Your Core Values: The Foundation of Your Product

In product management, understanding the core values of a product is essential to ensure it meets the needs of its users and stays true to its purpose. The same is true in life. Core values are the fundamental beliefs and principles that guide your behavior and decision-making. They are the foundation upon which you build your life, shaping everything from your goals and aspirations to your relationships and career choices.

Identifying your core values requires introspection and self-awareness. It involves asking yourself what truly matters to you, what you stand for, and what you're willing to fight for. These values aren't just abstract concepts—they're the driving force behind your actions and decisions.

For example, lets say integrity is one of your core values. Like the time you could have fudged your work hours but didn't—because your conscience, that annoying little thing, just wouldn't let you. This value will influence how you conduct yourself in both your personal and professional life. You'll prioritize honesty and transparency in your interactions with others and make decisions that align with this value, even when it's difficult. If you're faced with an ethical dilemma at work—like whether to report a mistake or overlook it to avoid conflict—your commitment to integrity will guide you to do the right thing, even if it's not the easiest option.

This chapter will explore how to identify your core values and how they can serve as the foundation of you as a product. We'll also look at aligning your actions and decisions with these values, ensuring that you stay true to yourself as you navigate the complexities of life.

First, take a moment to reflect on the following questions:

- What qualities do you admire most in others?
- What principles guide your decisions and actions?
- What are you most passionate about?
- When faced with a difficult decision, what values do you rely on to guide you?

Write down your answers and look for common themes. These themes will help you identify your core values. Once you have a list of values, prioritize them based on their importance to you. These values will guide you as you navigate life's challenges and opportunities. These questions are only the beginning.

When we consider what "value" means, we must recognize that there are layers or nuances we should consider. So, let's break down the intricacies of value.

Discovering, Creating, and Capturing Value

In product management, value isn't just a buzzword; it's a trifecta of principles that make or break a product: value discovery, value creation, and value capture. Yes, they might sound like different flavors of the same thing, but each one has a distinct role in creating a product that's worth its salt (and possibly even a sprinkle of pepper). When applied to life, these concepts help you understand what you truly care about, what you can contribute, and—perhaps most importantly—what you need to protect as you grow. Let's dig in.

1. Value Discovery: Finding Your "Why" (and Maybe a Few "Why Nots")

Value discovery is where a product manager channels their inner Sherlock Holmes, ferreting out the unmet needs and hidden desires of users. It's all about looking for clues, sometimes in the most unexpected places (like user complaints or, you know, your own life decisions that didn't quite pan out). For a product manager, this might involve endless user interviews and surveys to nail down what users truly value.

In life, value discovery is that same sleuthing process, but the user is you. What do you love doing (besides avoiding chores)? What kinds of activities and people make you feel alive? Reflecting on these questions is like panning for gold—you sift through the dirt of everyday routine until you find the little nuggets that genuinely matter. Take a hint from product managers: don't be afraid to get specific and question your assumptions. After all, you might discover your "non-negotiables" include morning coffee, an extra 15 minutes of sleep, and an undisturbed Netflix binge every Friday.

2. Value Creation: Putting Your Unique Skills to Work

Once you've unearthed what matters most, it's time to create some value. In the product world, this is where managers roll up their sleeves, take those user insights, and turn them into features people can't live without (or at least, can't complain about as much). It's about turning abstract ideas into something real.

In life, value creation means taking those insights about yourself and translating them into impact. Maybe you're a great listener (or at least pretend convincingly at parties). Why not use that skill to connect with others or mentor someone? Or if you're a whiz at solving puzzles, apply that to your job and become the office problem-solver. This is where you bring your A-game—and possibly your B-game, too—building on your strengths to contribute meaningfully. Like any product feature, you can refine and adjust these qualities over time, creating value not only for yourself but for others around you.

3. Value Capture: Holding onto What You've Built (No Hoarding Allowed)

Finally, value capture is about ensuring that all that hard-earned value doesn't just vanish into thin air. In product management, it means making sure users actually stick around, bringing in revenue or engagement. Think of it as putting up a "No Free Samples" sign—value has been created, now it needs to pay off.

In life, value capture is more about safeguarding what you've built and staying aligned with what's important. Have you developed a supportive friend group? Make time for them. Achieved a healthier lifestyle? Hold on to it by staying active (and maybe skipping that third slice of cake). Just as a product manager tracks retention, you can track your own priorities to make sure they stay part of your life. After all, what's the point of creating value if you're not keeping it around?

Value discovery, creation, and capture aren't just stages—they're a cycle. In life, as in product management, what you value might evolve over time, so it's worth revisiting these steps periodically. Discover what matters, make it real, and protect it. Rinse and repeat.

Reflection and Actionable Advice:

- Reflect on moments when you felt truly fulfilled—these can reveal what you value most (value discovery).
- Identify a personal strength and brainstorm ways to use it to positively impact others (value creation).
- Look at your life and ask, "What do I want to keep close, and how can I maintain it?" (value capture).

Now, let's look at how choices and value connect.

Behavioral Economics and Decision Science: Making Choices That Reflect Your Values

Understanding your core values is just the beginning. The next step is making decisions that align with these values, which can be challenging given the various biases and pressures we face. Behavioral economics and decision science provide tools to help you navigate these challenges.

One effective approach is **pre-commitment** — deciding in advance to limit your future options, thus ensuring your choices align with your values. For instance, if you value health, you might commit to a regular fitness routine by signing up for classes in advance, making it harder to skip out later.

Another helpful strategy is **choice architecture**—structuring your environment in a way that makes it easier to make value-aligned decisions. If spending quality time with family is important to you, design your home to facilitate that, such as creating spaces that encourage togetherness.

These tools help you make decisions that are consistent with your core values, ensuring that your actions reflect who you are and what you stand for. If we take it a step further, we must explore ethics.

Ethics in Personal Life: The Power of Doing the Right Thing

Ethical decision-making is about more than just adhering to moral principles; it's about making choices that align with your values and considering their long-term impact. When you make decisions with integrity, you build a foundation of trust in your relationships and strengthen your personal sense of self.

Consider the concept of **moral identity**—seeing yourself as someone who inherently values ethics and integrity. When this identity is central to your self-concept, you're more likely to make decisions that uphold these values, even in challenging situations.

Ethical choices also often involve considering the broader impact of your actions, including sustainability. Making decisions that not only benefit you but also consider the well-being of others and the environment can lead to a more balanced, fulfilling life. But how do you build a life based on core values?

Building Your Core Features

Just as a product has features that make it unique and valuable, you have strengths and qualities that define who you are and what you offer to the world. These core features are the aspects of your personality, skills, and experiences that set you apart and make you uniquely qualified to achieve your goals.

Identifying your core features requires an honest assessment of your strengths and weaknesses. It involves recognizing what you do well, where you excel, and what you bring to the table that others may not. It also includes acknowledging areas where you may need to improve or develop new skills.

For instance, say empathy is one of your core features. You've mastered the art of pretending to be interested in your friend's third retelling of their cat's latest escapade. I jest, but this quality allows you to connect with others on a deeper level, understand their needs, and respond in a supportive and compassionate way. Empathy can be a significant asset in your relationships and career, helping you build trust and rapport with those around you. However, if you struggle with time management, this might be an area where you need to develop new skills to ensure you can effectively meet your goals and responsibilities.

A real-life example of this concept is the story of Sarah, a young professional who recognized that her unique attribute was her ability to connect with people on a personal level. While others in her industry focused on technical skills, Sarah leveraged her empathy and communication skills to build strong client relationships. This not only helped her succeed in her career but also allowed her to make a significant impact in her community by leading initiatives that brought people together.

Another example is Mark, a mid-career professional who realized his core feature was his analytical mind. By honing his problem-solving skills and deepening his knowledge in his field, Mark was able to pivot his career from a generalist role to a specialized position where his unique strengths were highly valued. These examples illustrate how identifying and building on your core features can lead to greater success and fulfilment.

Of course, any discussion of core features must include the concept of resilience because setbacks are a certainty.

Resilience as a Core Feature

Resilience is one of the most important core features you can develop. Life is full of setbacks, and how you respond to them can make all the difference. Building resilience means developing the ability to bounce back from challenges, learn from failures, and keep moving forward. Think of it as being a human rubber band—no matter how many times life stretches you to the limit, you snap right back into shape. Just hopefully not into someone's eye.

The issue with building resilience is that fear often gets in the way. Many people avoid taking risks because they're afraid of making mistakes. However, this mindset can prevent you from growing and reaching your full potential. Failure is often seen as a negative experience, but it's actually one of the best teachers. When a product feature doesn't perform as expected, it provides insights that can lead to improvements.

Embracing failure as a natural part of the learning process is key to developing resilience. Think of a child learning to sit, crawl, walk, and eventually run. The process involves falling over, falling down, and many missed steps. But the child gets up and tries again, learning to adapt and adjust with each attempt.

By cultivating resilience, you can navigate life's ups and downs with confidence and grace. This core feature will help you stay focused on your goals, even when the going gets tough, and will ultimately lead to greater success and fulfilment.

Reflection and Actionable Advice:

- Reflect on a recent setback or failure. What did you learn from the experience, and how can you apply that knowledge going forward?
- Identify areas in your life where the fear of failure might be holding you back. Consider taking a small risk in one of these areas to practice building resilience.
- Celebrate your successes, but also recognize and appreciate the growth that comes from overcoming challenges.

Building core features and identifying value is rooted in self-reflection and awareness. So, we'd be remiss not to spend some time on the subject.

The Importance of Self-Awareness in Product Development

Self-awareness is the foundation of personal growth. In product management, understanding a product's strengths and weaknesses is essential for its development and success. The same principle applies to your personal life—knowing yourself deeply allows you to make informed decisions, build on your strengths, and address your weaknesses.

Just as a product manager conducts regular audits to assess a product's performance, you can perform a self-audit to evaluate where you stand in various aspects of your life—and no, unfortunately, life doesn't come with a GPS to help you avoid traffic jams or bad decisions. However, doing a self-audit could include assessing your emotional health, relationships, career, and personal goals. By identifying areas where you excel and those that need improvement, you can create a more targeted plan for personal development and work to redirect your traffic and avoid those late night bad decisions.

A common challenge with self-awareness is the tendency to avoid difficult truths about ourselves. It's easy to focus on our strengths while ignoring our weaknesses. However, true self-awareness requires honest reflection and a willingness to confront areas that need work. Avoiding this can lead to stagnation and missed opportunities for growth.

Reflection and Actionable Advice:

- Set aside time for regular self-reflection, whether through journaling, meditation, or discussions with a trusted friend or mentor.

- Be honest with yourself about your strengths and weaknesses. Use this awareness to guide your decisions and actions.
- Consider seeking feedback from others to gain a more objective view of your areas for improvement.

Chapter 3
Understanding the Market: Life's Challenges and Opportunities

In product management, understanding the market is crucial to ensuring that your product meets the needs of its users and achieves success. This involves conducting market research, analyzing competitors, and identifying opportunities for growth and innovation. Just as a product manager must understand the market to ensure a product's success, you must understand the "market" of your life—your environment, the challenges you face, and the opportunities available to you. This understanding allows you to navigate life's complexities with greater clarity and purpose. In life, the "market" is the world around you—the challenges, opportunities, and trends that influence your decisions and shape your path.

Understanding the market requires a deep awareness of your environment, your competition, and the opportunities available to you. It involves recognizing the challenges you face and finding ways to turn them into opportunities for growth and development.

Imagine you're facing a significant challenge at work, such as a demanding project or a difficult relationship with a colleague. Rather than viewing this challenge as an obstacle, you could see it as an opportunity to develop new skills, build resilience, and demonstrate your ability to handle adversity. By understanding the market—your work environment, your colleagues, and the demands of the project—you can identify ways to turn this challenge into a stepping stone for your career.

Creating a Product (Life) Vision

In product management, a vision is a clear and compelling picture of what the product aims to achieve. It's not just about where the product is today but where it needs to be in the future to meet the needs of its users and stand out in the market. A well-crafted vision acts as a guiding star, steering every decision, every feature, and every roadmap toward a common goal.

Similarly, in life, having a personal vision is essential. Your vision is your long-term aspiration, a mental image of the future you want to create for yourself. It provides direction, motivation, and a sense of purpose, helping you navigate the challenges and opportunities that come your way. Without a clear vision, you risk drifting aimlessly, reacting to life's events rather than shaping them.

Creating a personal vision begins with self-reflection. It's about understanding what truly matters to you, what you want to achieve, and the legacy you wish to leave behind. Your vision should encompass all areas of your life—career, relationships, health, personal growth, and contribution to the world. It's a holistic view of what a fulfilling life looks like for you.

Consider someone who envisions themselves as a successful

entrepreneur, a loving partner, a dedicated parent, and a contributor to their community. This vision isn't limited to their professional success; it also includes their personal relationships, health, and societal impact. Each of these areas is interconnected, and success in one often supports success in others. For instance, being a loving partner can provide emotional support that fuels professional success, while good health enables them to pursue their goals with energy and focus.

Aligning Your Vision with Your Core Values

Your personal vision should be deeply aligned with your core values—the principles and beliefs that guide your decisions and actions. When your vision reflects your values, it resonates more deeply and becomes a powerful motivator. For example, if one of your core values is "integrity," your vision might include being known for ethical leadership in your industry. If "creativity" is a core value, your vision might involve making a unique contribution to the arts or innovation in your field.

To begin crafting your personal vision, start by asking yourself these questions:

- What are the key areas of my life that I want to develop or achieve?
- What legacy do I want to leave behind?
- How do I want to be remembered by those closest to me?
- What are the values that are non-negotiable for me?

Once you've reflected on these questions, write a vision statement that encapsulates your aspirations. This statement should be specific enough to guide your actions but broad enough to allow for growth and change. Revisit and refine your vision statement regularly as you progress in your journey.

Translating Vision into Strategy

In product management, a vision alone isn't enough; it must be translated into a strategy—a high-level plan that outlines how the vision will be achieved. The strategy defines the path forward, identifying the key initiatives, priorities, and resources needed to bring the vision to life.

In your personal life, translating your vision into a strategy involves setting long-term goals and identifying the steps required to achieve them. This might include acquiring new skills, building relationships, or making lifestyle changes. The strategy should be flexible enough to adapt to new opportunities and challenges, yet clear enough to keep you on track.

Suppose your vision includes becoming a leader in your industry. Your strategy might involve pursuing advanced education, seeking mentorship, and building a network of professional contacts. You might also focus on developing specific leadership skills, such as decision-making and communication. By breaking down your vision into actionable steps, you create a roadmap for your journey. One way to do this is through a SWOT analysis.

Conducting a Personal SWOT Analysis

Nothing says 'I've got my life together like a SWOT analysis pinned to your fridge right next to the 'Best Pizza in Town' flyer. A SWOT analysis is a strategic tool used in product management to assess a product's strengths, weaknesses, opportunities, and threats. You can apply this same tool to your life to gain a better understanding of your current situation and identify areas for growth. Consider the following:

- **Strengths:** What are your greatest strengths? What do you do well?
- **Weaknesses:** Where do you see room for improvement? What challenges are you currently facing?
- **Opportunities:** What top opportunities are available to you? How can you leverage your strengths to take advantage of these opportunities?
- **Threats:** What external factors could potentially hinder your progress? How can you mitigate these threats?

Take some time to reflect on these questions and write down your answers. Use this analysis to develop a plan for leveraging your strengths, addressing your weaknesses, and seizing opportunities for growth.

Real-Life Examples of Navigating Life's Market

Consider John, a recent college graduate who conducted a personal SWOT analysis to better understand his place in the job market. By identifying his strengths in communication and his passion for technology, he was able to focus on roles that matched these attributes. He also recognized his lack of experience as a weakness, so he sought out internships and volunteer opportunities to build his resume. By leveraging his strengths and addressing his weaknesses, John successfully navigated the job market and landed a position that aligned with his goals. Now he can confidently say he's living the dream—well, minus the part where he still eats ramen noodles three times a week.

Another example is Lisa, a mid-career professional who used a SWOT analysis to evaluate her next career move. She identified an emerging trend in her industry that aligned with her skills and interests, representing a significant opportunity for growth. By positioning herself as an expert in this niche area, Lisa was able to transition into a new role that not only advanced her career but also reignited her passion for her work. Reflecting back, she realized she was one 'I need to speak to the manager' away from becoming a meme, so the career change was timely.

Setting Milestones and Tracking Progress

Just as a product manager sets milestones to track the progress of a product's development, you should establish milestones in your personal life to measure your progress toward your vision. Milestones are significant achievements or markers along the way that indicate you're on the right path. They provide motivation and a sense of accomplishment, helping you stay focused and energized.

If your vision is to become a recognized expert in your field, your milestones might include completing a degree or certification, publishing an article in a respected journal, or speaking at a major conference. Each of these milestones represents a step closer to your ultimate vision, and achieving them reinforces your commitment to your goals.

Take your vision and break it down into specific milestones. For each milestone, identify the actions you need to take and the timeline for achieving them. This could be a combination of short-term goals (e.g., completing a course within six months) and long-term goals (e.g., reaching a senior position within five years). Regularly review and adjust your milestone plan as you progress.

Navigating Challenges and Adapting Your Vision

Even the best-laid plans encounter obstacles. In product management, unforeseen challenges often require a pivot or adjustment in strategy to stay aligned with the vision. The same is true in life—unexpected events, changing circumstances, or new insights may lead you to revise your vision or strategy.

Adapting your vision doesn't mean abandoning your goals; rather, it involves being flexible and resilient, adjusting your course as needed while staying true to your core values. This adaptability is key to long-term success and fulfilment.

Imagine your vision involves starting your own business, but an economic downturn makes it difficult to secure funding. Rather than giving up, you might adapt your vision by focusing on building your skills, networking, or starting with a smaller, more manageable venture. This flexibility allows you to continue progressing toward your vision, even if the path looks different than you initially imagined.

Reflection and Actionable Advice:

- Regularly revisit and refine your vision to ensure it remains aligned with your values and circumstances.

- Set clear, actionable milestones to track your progress and celebrate your achievements along the way.
- Stay adaptable, recognizing that your vision may evolve as you grow and as external factors change.
- Use your vision as a decision-making tool, helping you stay focused on what truly matters and avoiding distractions or detours.

Crafting and maintaining a personal vision are one of the most powerful tools for navigating life with purpose and intention. By aligning your vision with your core values, translating it into a strategic plan, and staying adaptable in the face of challenges, you can create a life that is not only successful but also deeply fulfilling.

As you continue your journey, remember that your vision is not set in stone—it is a living, evolving guide that grows with you. Keep it front and center in your decisions, and let it inspire you to reach your highest potential.Bottom of Form

Chapter 4
Building Your Personal Product and Product Team

No product ever succeeds alone; it requires a team of dedicated individuals to bring it to life, refine it, and ensure its success in the market. The same principle applies to your personal growth and life journey. Think of the people around you as your "personal product team." Each person in your life plays a unique role, contributing to your growth, success, and well-being. Yes, even that one friend who insists on trying the weirdest food combinations, like peanut butter and pickles—hey, maybe they're onto something about looking at life differently! Understanding these roles and how to leverage them is crucial to building a strong support system. Maybe the world is better with a little more experimentation, just not at dinner.

So, let's first uncover what our product team looks like. From there, we will explore your product design.

Your Core Team: Friends and Family

Your friends and family are like the foundation of your personal product team. They're the ones who have been with you through thick and thin, supporting you, cheering you on, and occasionally telling you when you're being ridiculous—because let's face it, we all need that reality check sometimes. These are the people you can rely on for emotional support, advice, and a good laugh when life gets too serious.

Think about the role of a supportive friend or family member. Imagine you've just had a terrible day at work. Your project is behind schedule, your boss is breathing down your neck, and you're starting to doubt whether you're cut out for this job. Enter your supportive friend—the one who knows exactly how to cheer you up, whether it's with a hilarious meme, a heartfelt conversation, or simply sitting with you in comfortable silence. This friend plays a crucial role in helping you regain your confidence and perspective, reminding you that you're more than just your work struggles.

Then there's the specialists.

The Specialists are Colleagues and Mentors

Just as a product development team includes specialists like designers, engineers, and marketers, your personal product team should include colleagues and mentors who provide expertise and guidance in specific areas of your life. These are the people who help you navigate your career, offering advice, feedback, and opportunities for growth. They're like your professional GPS, helping you avoid career dead ends and guiding you toward success. Unlike your GPS, they won't keep telling you to "recalculate" every time you make a questionable life choice.

The Role of a Mentor in Career Transitions

Mentorship is one of the most valuable assets in any personal product team. A mentor is someone who has been where you want to go and can offer guidance, wisdom, and support as you navigate your career and personal development. But mentorship isn't just for when you're starting out—it's equally crucial during career transitions or when you're looking to pivot into a new field.

For example, imagine you're in a mid-career slump. You've been in the same role for years, and while you're comfortable, you're no longer challenged or excited about your work. A mentor who has navigated similar transitions can provide insights on how to reskill, identify new opportunities, and position yourself for a new role. They can also introduce you to key contacts in your desired field, providing a bridge between where you are and where you want to be.

Mentorship can take many forms—formal programs, informal advice, or even reverse mentoring, where a younger or less experienced person provides fresh perspectives to someone more senior. The key is to approach mentorship as a two-way street; it's about giving as much as you get, whether that's offering your time, skills, or simply being open to learning.

Reflection and Actionable Advice:

- Take stock of your personal product team. Who are

the key players in your life, and what roles do they play?

- Identify any gaps in your team. Are there areas where you could benefit from additional support or expertise?
- Consider reaching out to potential mentors or expanding your network to include people who can help you achieve your goals.

The Wild Cards or Unexpected Allies and Surprising Support

Sometimes, the people who end up being crucial to your personal product team aren't who you'd expect. Maybe it's that colleague you never thought you'd get along with, or the neighbor who always seems to know exactly when you need a pick-me-up. These wild cards can offer fresh views and perspective.

What if you're at a crossroads in your career, unsure whether to take a risky new job opportunity or stick with the devil you know? Out of nowhere, a casual acquaintance from your gym—whom you've barely exchanged more than a few "hello's" with—strikes up a conversation that turns into the most insightful career advice you've ever received. Turns out, this person has been in a similar situation and shares their story, which ends up guiding your decision. Who knew that your sweaty, post-workout self could attract such valuable guidance?

Reflection and Actionable Advice:

- Consider who in your life might be an unexpected ally. How can you open yourself up to their insights and support?
- Be mindful of the people you might overlook in your personal and professional life—they might just surprise you with the value they can offer.

Identifying your various team members and bringing them together is crucial because in product management, cross-functional teams come with different skills to work toward a common goal. In your personal life, collaborating with people outside your usual circles can lead to growth and innovation.

Think about how you've stuck to your routine, working with people who think like you. Then one day, you get assigned to a project with someone from a completely different department—or maybe even a different industry. You have nothing in common, except this project. At first, you clash over everything, from communication styles to ideas. But as the project progresses, you start to see the value in each other's perspectives. By the end, not only have you completed a successful project, but you've also expanded your own skill set and developed a newfound appreciation for diversity in thinking.

Reflection and Actionable Advice:

- Identify areas in your life where you might benefit from a cross-functional approach. This could be in your career, hobbies, or even in solving everyday challenges.

- Seek out opportunities to collaborate with people who bring different skills and perspectives to the table. These collaborations can be eye-opening and lead to unexpected success.

Now that you have your team, it's all about product design. There are three areas of focus. They are inclusivity, narrative, and emotion. Let's investigate each concept like your life product depends on it—because it does!

Inclusive Design: Creating Environments That Welcome Diverse Perspectives

Just as product managers strive to create products that are inclusive and accessible to all users, you should aim to build a personal environment that welcomes diverse perspectives. This means surrounding yourself with people who challenge your thinking, broaden your horizons, and encourage you to consider different viewpoints. Diversity isn't just about demographics; it's about having a range of experiences, ideas, and perspectives that enrich your life. We cannot create a unique self without exploring all the options. So, try the pineapple on pizza or go to a silent rave—the world offers vast perspectives and experiences to draw from.

Or course it is nice to have a close-knit group of friends who all share similar backgrounds, interests, and perspectives. However, this can create a sense of comfort and belonging, it can also lead to an echo chamber where your ideas and beliefs are rarely challenged. Now, imagine expanding your circle to include people from different cultures, professions, and walks of life. These new friendships can expose you to different ways of thinking, helping you grow as a person and make more informed decisions.

Creating Inclusive Social and Professional Environments

Building an inclusive environment in your life isn't just about who you know—it's about how you interact with them. Do you create spaces where people feel heard and valued? Are you open to ideas that differ from your own? Inclusive environments are built on the principles of respect, openness, and a genuine curiosity about the experiences of others.

In a professional setting, this might involve actively seeking out diverse voices in meetings, ensuring that everyone has a chance to contribute. In your personal life, it could mean being more intentional about the activities you engage in—choosing to attend events or join groups that bring together a variety of perspectives.

Reflection and Actionable Advice:

- Evaluate the diversity of your personal product team. Are you surrounded by people who challenge and inspire you, or do you need to broaden your circle?
- Seek out opportunities to connect with people who have different perspectives, whether through networking events, community activities, or online platforms.
- Embrace the discomfort that comes with being exposed to new ideas—it's a sign that you're growing and expanding your horizons.

Then consider narrative design.

Narrative Design: Crafting a Compelling Personal Story

In product management, narrative design is about creating a compelling story that resonates with users and draws them into the product experience. Similarly, in life, your personal story is a powerful tool for connecting with others, building relationships, and achieving your goals. The way you present yourself—your values, experiences, and aspirations—can shape how others perceive you and influence the opportunities that come your way.

Think of it as curating your life's highlight reel on social media—but, you know, without the pressure to filter out every imperfection.

When thinking of narrative design, consider the person who has overcome significant challenges in their life, such as a difficult upbringing or a major career setback. By crafting a narrative that highlights their resilience, determination, and growth, they can inspire others and build a reputation as someone who is capable and driven. This personal narrative becomes a key part of their identity, influencing how they are perceived by colleagues, mentors, and even potential employers.

Narrative design is about building a personal brand or reputation through storytelling. This personal narrative is a cornerstone of your personal brand or reputation and how you present yourself to the world. Just as companies use branding to communicate their values and differentiate themselves in the market, you can use your narrative to showcase who you are and what you stand for. This isn't about creating a facade; it's about being authentic and intentional in how you share your story.

For example, if you're passionate about environmental sustainability, weave that into your narrative. Share stories of how you've made eco-friendly choices in your life, whether it's through volunteering, advocacy, or simply making conscious consumer decisions. This not only reinforces your commitment to sustainability but also attracts like-minded individuals who share your values.

Think about the qualities you want to be known for—integrity, empathy, innovation, positivity. These shape how people see you and can have a HUGE impact on your career.

We all have to-do lists, but what if you created a "To-Be" list instead? A list that focuses on the qualities you want to embody and the person you want to become. When you're clear on WHO you want to be and the qualities you want to embody, your actions naturally align. So, what's on your "To Be" list? How do you want to show up in your professional life?

Reflection and Actionable Advice:

- Reflect on your life experiences and the lessons you've learned. How can you craft these into a compelling personal narrative that highlights your strengths and values?
- Share your story with others, whether through conversations, social media, or professional platforms. Your narrative can inspire and connect with others, opening doors to new opportunities.
- Remember that your narrative is an ongoing story. As you grow and evolve, continue to refine and update

your story to reflect your current goals and aspirations.

Now, let's explore emotion through emotional design.

Emotional Design and Building Emotional Connections in Relationships

Emotional design in product management is about creating products that evoke positive emotions and build strong connections with users. In your personal life, building emotional connections with others is equally important. These connections are the glue that holds your personal product team together, fostering trust, loyalty, and mutual support.

Remember that time you called your best friend at 2 AM to rant about your latest life crisis, and they picked up on the first ring? That's emotional design in action—minus the UX jargon.

Think about a time when you were going through a tough time, whether it was a personal loss, a career setback, or just the general stress of life. A friend reaches out to you, not with solutions or advice, but simply to listen and empathize with what you're going through. This act of empathy strengthens your emotional connection, making you feel valued and understood. Just as a well-designed product evokes positive emotions in its users, these emotional connections in your relationships create a sense of belonging and support.

Building emotional connections doesn't require grand gestures or dramatic expressions of affection. Often, it's the small, consistent acts of kindness and empathy that build the strongest bonds. This could be something as simple as remembering a friend's favorite snack and bringing it to them when they're having a rough day or sending a quick message to check in on someone you haven't heard from in a while.

Another strategy is active listening—really focusing on what the other person is saying, without interrupting or thinking about your response. Active listening shows that you value the other person's thoughts and feelings, and it helps build trust and mutual respect in your relationships.

Reflection and Actionable Advice:

- Focus on building deeper emotional connections with the people in your life. This might involve being more present in your interactions, showing empathy, and being vulnerable about your own experiences.
- Consider how you can create positive emotional experiences for others, whether through acts of kindness, thoughtful gestures, or simply being a good listener.
- Remember that emotional design is an ongoing process. Continuously invest in your relationships to build and maintain strong emotional connections.

These three product design concepts are inward focused. They highlight what you can do and what you have control over. However, this is only half of the puzzle. In product management, one must consider the user and their willingness to adopt the product. This is called the product adoption curve.

Understanding the Product Adoption Curve

The product adoption curve is a model that categorizes consumers into five segments based on their willingness to adopt new products or ideas: innovators, early adopters, early majority, late majority, and laggards. This curve is crucial for product managers to understand how to market products effectively and manage their lifecycle. Similarly, in your personal life, recognizing these categories among your "users"—the people in your life—can help you navigate relationships, influence decisions, and foster personal growth. Product success depends on user adoption. For example, you might not take a laggard to fainting goat yoga but consider the early adopter; they are innovators and risk takers!

Innovators and Early Adopters: The Visionaries in Your Life

Innovators are the risk takers, the ones who are always on the lookout for the latest trends and ideas. In your personal life, these are the friends or colleagues who encourage you to try new things, push your boundaries, and embrace change. They're the ones who convinced you to try that new meditation app or sign up for that improv class.

Early adopters are similar but slightly more cautious. They're quick to adopt new ideas once they see the value, but they still need some convincing. These individuals are your allies when you're looking to implement a new habit or start a new venture—they'll join you once you've taken the first step.

Think about a time when you were hesitant to try something new, like adopting a new technology or changing your routine. Who in your life encouraged you to give it a shot? These are your innovators and early adopters—people who are open to new ideas and can help you explore uncharted territory.

Then there are the early and late majority.

The Early and Late Majority (Steady Builders)

The early majority are the pragmatists. They wait until there's some evidence that a new idea works before they jump on board. They're not the first to adopt, but once they do, they help build momentum. In your personal life, these might be the friends or colleagues who support your new endeavors once they see that it's working out for you.

In close second is the late majority who are more skeptical and need to see widespread adoption before they're willing to change. They might be the family members who finally switch to a smartphone years after everyone else or the colleague who's hesitant to adopt new software until it's company-wide policy.

Consider a time when you tried to introduce a new idea at work or among your friends. Who were the ones who waited to see how it worked out before they joined in? Electric car or Pilates anyone? Understanding who these people are can help you strategize how to present new ideas or changes in a way that resonates with them.

Then you have the laggards.

Laggards or Traditionalists

Laggards are the last to adopt new ideas, often clinging to

tradition and familiarity. In your personal life, these might be the people who resist change the most. They're not necessarily negative; they just need more time and assurance before they're ready to embrace something new.

Think about the people in your life who are resistant to change. How have you managed to bring them along on your journey? Sometimes, it requires patience, persistence, and a lot of evidence to convince them that a new approach is worth trying. Sounds like showing grandma how to use Facetime in 2020!

Each of these categories—innovators, early adopters, early majority, late majority, and laggards—plays a role in your personal growth and development. Innovators and early adopters can help you push boundaries and try new things, while the early and late majority provide stability and support as you implement changes. Laggards, though resistant, can help you refine your ideas and approaches, ensuring they're solid and sustainable before widespread adoption.

Reflection and Actionable Advice:

- Identify the innovators, early adopters, early majority, late majority, and laggards in your life. How do they influence your decisions and growth?
- Consider how you can leverage the strengths of each group to support your personal and professional development.
- Reflect on how you interact with each group. Are there ways to better communicate and engage with them to foster positive change?

Up to now, we have considered team, product design, and users—all from a positive perspective. However, what happens when your product (you) isn't adopted?

The Role of Critics and Conflicts:

Everyone's a critic—at some point. We all have that one friend or colleague who never sugarcoats anything. While their bluntness can sometimes sting, they're often the ones who help you see things from a different angle. Maybe they're the person who told you that your brilliant idea wasn't so brilliant after all—but instead of being defensive, you took their advice, made some tweaks, and ended up with a far better result. Thanks Mom!

Every product team has its critics, and so does your personal product team. Critics can be incredibly valuable, providing the kind of feedback that no one else dares to give. The trick is knowing how to take this feedback in stride and use it for your growth.

Additionally, no team is without conflict, and your personal product team is no exception. Learning how to navigate disagreements is essential for maintaining harmony and moving forward.

Have you ever had a heated debate with a friend or colleague where neither of you is willing to back down, and the conversation is going nowhere? Instead of letting the disagreement damage your relationship, you decide to agree to disagree. You respect each other's viewpoints and move on, stronger for having had the conversation. Perhaps, politicians could learn something or use the following advice!

Reflection and Actionable Advice:

- Embrace the critics in your life. Understand that their feedback, while tough to hear, can lead to significant growth and improvement.
- Learn to differentiate between constructive criticism and negativity. Focus on the feedback that helps you grow and ignore the rest.
- Recognize that conflict is a natural part of any relationship or team. It's how you handle it that matters.
- Practice the art of agreeing to disagree. Not every argument needs a winner—sometimes, it's enough to understand where the other person is coming from.

Of course, identifying and working with your product team, determining your product design, and learning to embrace critics and conflict is only the beginning. At some point, you must execute and introduce your product. You need a plan, and that plan starts with setting and measuring goals. Afterall, you can't take that trip to Tahiti without proper planning and execution, right?

Chapter 5
The Wonderful World of KPIs

When you think of KPIs (Key Performance Indicators) in product management, you might imagine a dashboard brimming with numbers, charts, and metrics—measuring everything from user retention to revenue growth. Product managers live and breathe KPIs because they provide tangible insights into whether a product is succeeding—or flopping—based on measurable outcomes. In product management, KPIs offer a way to track progress, course-correct when necessary, and make data-driven decisions to push the product forward. But here's the thing: KPIs aren't just for products. You can use them in your personal life too—only your KPIs will probably look a bit different (unless your life goals revolve around customer acquisition, in which case, go you!).

KPIs in Product Management: The Basics

In product management, KPIs act as a compass, guiding the product team and stakeholders on whether they're moving in the right direction. They measure critical aspects of product performance like:

- **Customer Retention Rate:** How many users stick around after downloading or purchasing your product? If your product is a sandwich shop, this KPI would be the number of regular customers who keep coming back for your special tuna melt. Spoiler alert: if it's not a lot, you've got some tweaking to do.
- **Monthly Active Users (MAU):** How many people are regularly using your product? If you're managing an app, this KPI tells you how engaging it is. Are people logging in daily? Or have they left it gathering digital dust in a folder on their phone?
- **Customer Satisfaction Score (CSAT):** How happy are your users? This is the "thumbs up" or "thumbs down" of product management. Think of it like your Uber rating—except you don't get candy points for being chatty with the driver.
- **Revenue Growth:** Are the dollars flowing in? A key metric for any business, tracking revenue tells you if the product is financially sustainable. If your product is bleeding cash, it might be time to hit pause on the confetti cannons.

These KPIs give product managers a real-time snapshot of how the product is doing and what needs attention. They are like the GPS of product management—without them, you're just driving aimlessly, hoping to end up somewhere good. But these metrics aren't just numbers. They inform decisions, guide priorities, and ultimately help steer the entire team toward success.

KPIs in Your Personal Life: A Different Spin

Now, let's step away from dashboards and focus on you, the product of your own life. Not all KPIs involve numbers—because, let's be real, if you tried to quantify happiness, it would probably look like a complicated graph involving puppies, pizza, and naps. Personal KPIs work in much the same way as product KPIs—they help you track progress, see where adjustments are needed, and celebrate wins. However, the metrics in your life are often a little more... human. They won't involve revenue or user growth (unless your dream is to become an influencer, then by all means, track those likes), but they'll still be focused on things that matter to you.

For example:

- **Health KPIs:** This could be how many times a week you hit the gym, how many hours of sleep you get, or how much water you drink daily. Your MAU (Monthly Active Uplifting Workouts) might measure how often you get out of bed and break a sweat—if your gym attendance is as sporadic as a one-hit wonder, it might be time to re-evaluate.
- **Happiness KPIs:** How often do you feel joy? Are you laughing enough? (If not, might I recommend some more memes?) You could track the number of hours you spend on activities that make you genuinely happy, like spending time with loved ones or reading your favorite book.

- **Relationship KPIs:** How often are you connecting meaningfully with the people who matter to you? This could be the number of times you've had a heart-to-heart conversation with a friend or set aside time for date night. If your emotional bandwidth feels stretched thin, your KPI for quality connections might need some adjustment.

Just like in product management, personal KPIs give you tangible ways to measure success. The key difference is that, while product KPIs are all about the performance of a product, personal KPIs are about how you're showing up for yourself and the people around you.

Set an emotional KPI around your happiness—like how often you feel joy in a day. Maybe it's laughing at memes, spending time with loved ones, or that first sip of coffee in the morning (the real MVP). If you start noticing that your happiness KPI spikes when you're around certain people—or plummets when you're doing certain activities—those are the things to prioritize (or avoid, like that weird tuna casserole your friend keeps bringing to potlucks).

If (by chance) you are a product manager, emotional KPIs can apply to your team, too. Instead of just tracking how many bugs get fixed, track the team's morale. Happy teams = better products. If your team's emotional KPI takes a nosedive during endless meetings or unrealistic deadlines, it's time to reassess. After all, a miserable team isn't going to produce their best work —no matter how many free snacks you offer.

Emotional KPIs remind us that life (and work) isn't just about hitting targets—it's about enjoying the journey. And maybe eating a lot of pizza along the way.

Reflection and Actionable Advice:

- Identify emotional KPIs that reflect your well-being, such as happiness, stress levels, or work-life balance.
- Track these emotional KPIs regularly to understand what contributes to your overall happiness and what detracts from it.
- Use this information to make adjustments in your life that prioritize your emotional well-being.

The Overlap: Comparing Product and Personal KPIs

The fascinating part? There's a surprising amount of overlap between product and personal KPIs. Both are about measuring what matters and using those measurements to guide decisions. The trick is understanding that while product KPIs might focus more on business metrics, personal KPIs focus on things like well-being, fulfilment, and growth. Let's break it down:

- **Retention Rate:** For a product manager, retention is about keeping users hooked. In life, retention might mean maintaining healthy relationships, sticking to habits, or staying consistent with goals. The principles are the same—are you keeping what's important close, or is it slipping away?
- **Growth Rate:** In product management, this might be revenue or user growth, but in life, it's about personal growth. Are you developing new skills? Taking steps toward a long-term goal? Whether it's financial

growth or spiritual growth, this KPI measures progress toward your bigger vision.

- **Satisfaction Score:** Product managers track user satisfaction, but in life, you should be tracking your own. How satisfied are you with your work, your relationships, your health? If your personal CSAT (Customer Satisfaction) is low, it might be time to reassess how you're spending your time.

Both types of KPIs help you make adjustments along the way. If the product—or you—aren't hitting the mark, it's time to pivot (more on that later in the chapter!). Whether you're running a company or just trying to run your life, the core principle is the same: measure what matters and let that data guide you.

Reflection and Actionable Advice:

KPIs offer a tangible way to measure success in both product management and life. They're not the end-all-be-all, but they do provide a clear snapshot of progress. So set some KPIs for yourself, but remember—life isn't a spreadsheet. Consider the following:

- **Identify Your Personal KPIs**
- Take some time to think about the areas in your life where you'd like to see growth or change. What truly matters to you? Is it improving your health, boosting your career, or enhancing your relationships? Define KPIs that will help you measure progress in these areas. Remember, KPIs aren't one-size-fits-all; they

should be meaningful and personalized to reflect what success looks like for you.

- **Make Your KPIs Tangible**
- Once you've identified your KPIs, ensure they're specific and measurable. For instance, if one of your personal KPIs is to improve your well-being, you might track the number of hours you dedicate to self-care each week. Make your KPIs something you can quantify and monitor regularly.
- **Balance Quantitative and Qualitative KPIs**
- While numbers are great, not all progress can be measured with a stat. Include qualitative KPIs that reflect experiences, feelings, and achievements. For example, tracking how often you feel happy or fulfilled during the week can be just as valuable as the number of projects you complete.
- **Track Progress Regularly**
- Make it a habit to check in on your KPIs. This could be weekly, monthly, or at a cadence that works best for you. Regularly tracking your KPIs helps you see trends over time, spot areas where you're excelling, and identify aspects that may need adjustment.
- **Adapt and Refine as Needed**
- KPIs aren't set in stone. Life changes, and so should your measures of success. If you notice that a particular KPI isn't serving its purpose, don't be afraid to tweak or replace it. Keep your KPIs aligned with your evolving priorities and goals.
- **Celebrate Milestones Along the Way**
- When you reach a key KPI milestone, take time to celebrate. Recognizing your progress not only boosts

motivation but also reinforces the positive habits that got you there. Whether it's a small treat or a fun activity, celebrating your KPIs is about acknowledging the steps you're taking toward your bigger picture.

KPIs are more than just numbers; they're a reflection of what's important to you and are a guide for how to get there. By regularly evaluating and refining your personal KPIs, you'll be able to track your journey in a way that feels meaningful and rewarding.

Chapter 6
A Practical Guide to Goal Setting

Now that you've got the lowdown on KPIs, it's time to talk about how to set goals that will get you to where you want to go—whether that's climbing the corporate ladder, running a marathon, or simply surviving the workday without needing a nap.

SMART and PACT Goals

We've all heard of SMART goals: Specific, Measurable, Achievable, Relevant, and Time-bound. It's the gold standard of goal setting, right? But what if I told you there's another framework that might be a better fit for certain situations? Enter PACT goals—Purposeful, Actionable, Continuous, and Trackable. While both could be used in product management, we often see an emphasis on life or personal goals. Let's compare these two approaches to see where each shine.

Now, let's break them down and see what SMART and PACT goals look like in the wild.

SMART Goals

In product management, setting SMART goals is like giving your team a treasure map—except instead of hunting for gold, they're hunting for bug fixes and feature rollouts. You've got a clear destination, checkpoints along the way, and a deadline to boot. For instance:

Objective: Improve the user sign-up experience to increase conversion rates by 15% within the next quarter.

- **Specific:** We're focusing on the sign-up process, not, say, redesigning the entire app because one user's cat didn't like it.
- **Measurable:** A 15% increase in conversion rates—because if we don't measure it, how will we know if we're winning?
- **Achievable:** Based on previous data and our caffeine consumption, this is totally doable.
- **Relevant:** People signing up = business growth. No sign-ups = lots of sad faces.
- **Time-bound:** We've got three months to pull this off. So, let's channel our inner action movie montage and get moving.

SMART goals help ensure that everyone on the team knows exactly what needs to happen and by when, so there's less ambiguity and more action. But how does this translate to life?

The example below shows the goal of losing ten pounds in

three months. It is SPECIFIC, MEASUREABLE, and TIME-BOUND. However, is it achievable and relevant? The last two are where many get caught in the weeds. Taking the time to identify the relevance and whether it is achievable is crucial or it will lead to another failed attempt. You can track progress through the suggested KPIs.

Now, let's explore PACT goals.

PACT Goals

In product management, PACT goals are for when you need to embrace the ebb and flow of an ongoing project—kind of like managing a garden, where you're more focused on nurturing growth than just getting the flowers to bloom now. It's all about being in it for the long haul. Here's an example.

Objective: Cultivate a continuous user feedback loop to guide ongoing product refinements.

- **Purposeful:** We're not just tweaking things randomly. We're actually using feedback—no more throwing darts in the dark!
- **Actionable:** We'll check in with our users bi-weekly, like catching up with an old friend—except this friend might tell us all the ways our product is driving them nuts.
- **Continuous:** This isn't a one-and-done deal. We're in it for the long game, always improving, like a never-ending Netflix series.
- **Trackable:** We'll track improvements based on user feedback—just like when you track how many

times your favorite show gets better after season three.

PACT goals are great when you want flexibility, iteration, and continuous improvement (more to come on iteration and improvement). They're more about the journey than the destination, and perfect when you're building long-term strategies or habits. Let's translate this to life.

The goal to cultivate a lifelong habit of exercise might seem a little wishy-washy because it isn't a hard line in the sand like losing ten pounds. However, that is where PACT goals shines. It is about being more fluid with purpose and taking continuous actions that are trackable.

So, whether focused on product management or personal goals, the question becomes: how do you choose which method to use? Keep the following in mind:

Use SMART Goals When:

- **Outcome-focused:** You have a clear, specific result you want to achieve (like fitting into those jeans or saving up for that vacation).
- **Project-based:** The goal is tied to something with an end date (like completing a home renovation or learning a new skill by the end of the year).
- **Time-sensitive:** The goal has a deadline, and you need to measure progress (like finishing a course or training for a 5K).

Example: Saving $1,000 in 6 months for a dream vacation. You have a set target and a deadline, so SMART goals are the way to go.

Use PACT Goals When:

- **Process-focused:** You're more concerned with building habits that last (like exercising regularly or eating healthier).
- **Habit-building:** The goal is to establish routines rather than achieve a single result (like meditating daily or reading more).
- **Flexibility needed:** You want to leave room to adjust as you grow (like improving your overall well-being or learning a new hobby).

Example: Developing a habit of daily meditation. It's not about how much you meditate, but that you make it a regular part of your life, which is perfect for PACT goals.

Both SMART and PACT goals have their place in personal development. SMART goals are great when you need to hit a specific target by a certain time, while PACT goals are better for long-term habits and continuous improvement. The best part? You can mix and match these frameworks depending on what you're trying to achieve. By understanding when and how to use each, you can set yourself up for success in both the short and long term, with ones that keep you motivated, whether you're trying to drop a few pounds, run a marathon, or just feel better every day.

Reflection and Actionable Advice:

- Start by defining what success looks like for you in various areas of your life—career, relationships, health, personal growth, etc.
- Identify specific, measurable KPIs that will help you track your progress toward these goals. Remember to include both quantitative (the hard numbers) and qualitative (the quality) measures.
- Regularly review your KPIs and adjust them as needed to ensure they continue to reflect your evolving goals and priorities.

Which every goal method you decide to use, you will be applying decision theory. So, let's talk about it!

Applying Decision Theory to Personal Goal Setting

Decision science or decision theory is the study of how people make decisions, particularly under conditions of uncertainty. In product management, decision theory is used to optimize product strategies and make informed choices. In your personal life, applying decision science can help you make better decisions, especially when it comes to setting and achieving your goals. It's like being your own life coach—but without the exorbitant fees or the awkward affirmations.

One decision science technique is precommitment—making a commitment to a course of action in advance to limit your future choices and avoid temptation. For example, if one of your goals is to exercise regularly, you might pre-commit by scheduling workouts with a friend, signing up for a fitness class, or laying out your workout clothes the night before. By reducing the need for decision-making in the moment, you increase the likelihood of sticking to your goals.

Of course, sticking to goals means you must have priorities. If not, then everything becomes a priority. So, consider the Eisenhower Matrix to help determine urgency.

Using the Eisenhower Matrix to Prioritize Tasks

In product management, you're constantly balancing competing priorities—bug fixes, feature development, customer requests, and business goals. The Eisenhower Matrix helps product managers make sense of the chaos by organizing tasks based on urgency and importance, ensuring that the team is focusing on what will drive the most value for the product and the business. The Eisenhower Matrix is a decision-making tool that helps you prioritize tasks based on their urgency and importance. It's divided into four quadrants:

1. **Urgent and Important:** Tasks you should do immediately.
2. **Important but Not Urgent:** Tasks you should schedule for later.
3. **Urgent but Not Important:** Tasks you should delegate if possible.
4. **Not Urgent and Not Important:** Tasks you should consider eliminating.

In personal life, this matrix helps you focus on what truly matters and avoid getting bogged down by less important tasks. But this tool also has significant relevance in product management, where prioritization is key to managing complex projects and ensuring that the most impactful work gets done.

Let's break down how each quadrant applies:

1. Urgent and Important (Do Now)

These are the tasks that demand immediate attention, typically because they are critical to the product's functionality or the business's success. In product management, this could include:

- **Critical Bugs or System Failures:** If a major bug is causing users to abandon the product or preventing them from completing key tasks, fixing this issue becomes the top priority. Delaying it could result in loss of customers, revenue, or both.
- **Deadline-Driven Deliverables:** Tasks related to upcoming product launches, investor meetings, or marketing campaigns also fall into this category. Missing these deadlines could severely impact the business.

In personal life, this might look like dealing with a health emergency or completing a major project due tomorrow. In both contexts, the focus is on tasks that simply can't wait without significant negative consequences.

2. Important but Not Urgent (Schedule for Later)

These tasks are crucial for long-term success but don't need to be completed right away. In product management, this quadrant is often where strategic thinking and planning come into play. Examples include:

- **Long-Term Feature Development:** Features that align with the product's vision and long-term strategy but aren't immediately required by users. These features might be game-changers down the road but can be scheduled for later.
- **User Research and Data Analysis:** Understanding your users is key to making informed product decisions, but this research doesn't always have a looming deadline. Scheduling time to analyze user behavior or conduct surveys helps ensure the product evolves in line with customer needs, but it's not an immediate fire.

In life, this quadrant includes tasks like career planning, learning new skills, or scheduling regular exercise—all important but not urgent today.

3. Urgent but Not Important (Delegate if Possible)

In product management, many tasks demand immediate attention but don't necessarily require the product manager's involvement. These tasks are prime candidates for delegation to team members, allowing the product manager to focus on more strategic issues. Examples include:

- **Routine Administrative Work:** While tasks like updating project tracking software or attending nonessential meetings might be necessary, they don't directly contribute to the product's success. A product manager might delegate these to an assistant or junior team member.

- **Customer Support Requests:** If a customer is facing an issue that's not critical to the product's overall function, handling it can be delegated to the support or customer success team. The product manager should stay informed but doesn't need to be hands-on with every request.

Think of this as those "urgent" but minor requests in life—such as handling small favors for others or low-priority emails—that can be passed off or managed with minimal direct involvement.

4. Not Urgent and Not Important (Eliminate)

In product management, tasks in this quadrant are often distractions that don't align with the product's goals or user needs. Eliminating or deprioritizing them is key to ensuring the team's time is used efficiently. Examples include:

- **Feature Creep:** Sometimes stakeholders or customers request features that sound good on paper but don't align with the product's vision or the users' actual needs. Instead of allocating resources to build these features, a product manager should eliminate them from the roadmap or push them to a much later stage.

- **Endless Tweaks to Non-Critical Features:** It's easy to get caught up in tweaking minor elements of a product, such as UI details that don't impact functionality. These tasks often don't move the needle for users and can be eliminated or postponed indefinitely.

Outside the office, think about those tasks that are not urgent or important. Is responding to gossip girls on social media really worth it?

Reflection and Actionable Advice:

- Identify areas where you struggle to stick to your goals. How can you use precommitment strategies to reduce the temptation to stray from your path?
- Consider other decision science techniques, such as setting default options or creating decision rules, to help you make more consistent progress toward your goals.
- Remember that decision science is about making your life easier, not harder. Focus on strategies that simplify your decision-making process and increase your chances of success.
- Evaluate your tasks using the Eisenhower Matrix and prioritize your efforts to ensure that you're spending time on what truly matters.
- Delegate where possible, and don't be afraid to eliminate tasks that don't contribute meaningfully to your goals—whether personal or professional.

So, you've set your goals and priorities, but such is life—you get thrown a curve ball or your plan isn't working like you thought it would. Now what?!

Pivoting Goals: When to Change Direction

Setting goals feels like plotting out a flawless master plan, but the truth is, life and product management often don't play by the rules. Whether you're managing a product or just managing life, knowing when to pivot is essential. Plans are great, but sticking to them no matter what? Not so much. Sometimes, new information or circumstances require a complete change of direction. The magic happens when you learn to adapt, making flexibility your new best friend.

Adaptability

In product management, adaptability is everything. You might have the perfect roadmap for a product launch, but what happens when user feedback, market conditions, or technology shifts throw your plan off course? You pivot. You adjust. The same principle applies to life. Maybe you've set a career or personal goal, but halfway through, you realize it's no longer fulfilling or realistic. Instead of grinding through a plan that no longer serves you, it's better to adapt and realign.

Let's talk about the marshmallow experiment, not the one where kids had to resist eating a marshmallow (though that's fun too). In this version, groups of architects, engineers, business students, and kindergarteners were given twenty pieces of spaghetti, a yard of tape, and one marshmallow. Their task? Build the tallest structure that could support the marshmallow on top. Guess who did the best?

Nope, not the business students or even the architects—it was the kindergarteners. Why? Because they didn't overthink it or plan obsessively. Instead, they built multiple prototypes, tested them, and adapted their designs along the way. They weren't afraid to fail and pivot. Meanwhile, the grown-ups focused on planning and theoretical structures, often leading to failure when their one big idea collapsed under the weight of that marshmallow.

The Lesson: You can plan meticulously, but if you're not testing, iterating, and adapting along the way, your "big idea" might crash and burn. Flexibility beats rigid planning every time, whether you're constructing a skyscraper or managing your personal goals. Planning is great, but acting, adjusting, and building on what you learn is better.

This "big idea flop" isn't a stranger to product management. Many times, a product team sets out to develop a shiny new feature. They spend weeks planning, mapping out every detail, and perfecting the design. But once it's launched, user feedback reveals that the feature isn't quite what they needed. What now? Like those kindergarteners, they need to adapt quickly—take the feedback, iterate, and make improvements. They don't let the marshmallow topple the whole project because they were too attached to the original plan.

This applies not only to product development but also to life. You can have the perfect career plan or fitness goal, but if you're not willing to adjust as new information comes in, your plan can quickly become obsolete. For example, let's say you've mapped out a five-year plan to become a marketing executive. You've plotted every step, from gaining experience to networking and getting certifications. But halfway through, you realize that you no longer enjoy marketing and want to pursue a career in design. What do you do? Do you stick to the original plan, or do you pivot? Much like the marshmallow experiment, success comes from building prototypes and adjusting as you go. If the plan isn't working, don't be afraid to scrap it and try something new.

How to Know When to Pivot

Just like in the marshmallow experiment, sometimes the structure you've built won't hold. That's when it's time to pivot. Here are a few signs that product managers use:

- **Stagnation:** If you've been grinding away at a goal and nothing's moving, it might be time to ask why. Is it still the right goal? Or is it time to shift gears?
- **Changing Circumstances:** In product management, market conditions change, competitors evolve, and technology advances. The same applies to your personal life—priorities shift, opportunities emerge, and new challenges arise. When the environment changes, so should your goals.
- **Feedback Loops:** In the marshmallow experiment, kindergarteners succeeded because they created feedback loops. They tested, observed, and adjusted. Whether it's user feedback in product development or personal feedback from experiences, these loops are critical. Listen to what the data—or life—is telling you.

The art of the pivot is invaluable. Goals aren't meant to be set in stone—they're meant to evolve with you. So, the next time your goal structure starts wobbling under the weight of life's marshmallows, remember it's okay to adjust, iterate, and pivot your way to success. In both life and product management, the key is recognizing when your current path isn't yielding the desired results and having the courage to pivot. This flexibility ensures that you're always moving toward something that truly aligns with your values and objectives, rather than sticking with a plan that no longer serves you.

Micro-Goals Make Pivoting Easier

Big goals are like trying to eat an entire pizza in one sitting—totally possible, but not advisable. Instead, micro-goals are the slice-by-slice approach. Each bite is manageable, and before you know it, you've conquered that pizza (or, you know, that big goal). However, these micro-goals change shape depending on whether we focus on product management or life.

For Example, a product manager wants to launch a huge feature, but if they try to do it all at once, chaos will reign. Instead, they break it down into smaller goals: first, gather user feedback; next, sketch out wireframes; then, start developing. It's like building the feature one Lego brick at a time—satisfying, manageable, and much less likely to result in a meltdown. Each step builds on the last, and before you know it, you're launching that killer feature (and probably celebrating with pizza, because why not?).

However, in life, these micro goals may not be so dependent on your paycheck. Say you've got this dream of writing a book, but the idea of sitting down and cranking out 80,000 words makes you rethink your life choices. Solution? Micro-goals!

Today, just write 500 words. Next week, finish one chapter. It's like slowly eating that pizza, one slice at a time, and enjoying the process. Each small win builds momentum—and keeps you from total word-count-induced paralysis.

Micro-goals keep you motivated and let you celebrate the small victories, like getting halfway through a pizza without regret (and saving room for dessert).

Reflection and Actionable Advice:

- Regularly assess your goals to ensure they still align with your values and aspirations.
- Don't be afraid to change direction if your goals no longer bring you satisfaction or joy.
- Embrace the flexibility of goal-setting. It's not about rigidly sticking to a plan; it's about finding the path that truly fulfills you.
- Test and iterate. Just like the marshmallow experiment showed, rapid iteration beats long planning. In your life, this means testing your ideas and adjusting them as you go. Don't wait for the perfect moment; take action and adapt based on the results.
- Balance planning with adaptability. Set goals and plan, but leave room for flexibility. Be willing to pivot if things aren't working, and use feedback (whether from others or from life itself) to guide your next move.
- Act on new information. Don't be afraid to change direction when the circumstances shift. Plans are important, but they're only useful if they stay

relevant. As new information comes in, use it to refine your path forward.

- Break down your big goals into smaller, actionable steps.
- Celebrate each micro-goal you achieve as a victory in its own right.
- Use micro-goals to maintain momentum and stay motivated on your journey to achieving larger goals.

Now, for those times that we can't see the forest for the trees, we need accountability partners in product management and life. So, it's worth given the concept a few words.

Accountability Partners: Keeping on Track

You've probably heard the saying, "It takes a village," and while that's usually in reference to raising kids, it applies just as well to managing your goals—whether in product management or in life. Accountability partners are like your personal cheerleaders, guiding you toward your objectives, and sometimes giving you a little nudge (or a swift kick) when you start to lose focus.

But what exactly is an accountability partner, and why are they so effective? Simply put, an accountability partner is someone who holds you to your commitments. They help keep you on track, remind you of your goals, and provide support when the going gets tough. Research has shown that having accountability partners can significantly increase your chances of achieving your goals—because let's face it, it's a lot harder to let things slide when someone else is checking in on your progress.

Accountability Partners in Product Management

In product management, accountability is key to ensuring that projects run smoothly and goals are met. Product managers juggle a lot of responsibilities, from guiding product development to managing stakeholder expectations. Having accountability partners can make all the difference. But who can fill this role for a product manager? Let's take a look at the possible players:

- **Supervisors or Senior Managers:** A supervisor or senior manager is often an obvious accountability partner for a product manager. They provide oversight, offer strategic guidance, and expect regular updates on the progress of the product. This creates a built-in structure of accountability, as product managers are required to meet deadlines, present results, and adjust course based on feedback. In many organizations, product managers have regular one-on-one check-ins with their supervisors, where progress is discussed and next steps are planned.
- **Mentors:** A mentor offers a more informal type of accountability. Unlike a supervisor, a mentor isn't necessarily involved in the day-to-day management of a product, but they can offer valuable advice, guidance, and perspective on broader career and product goals. A mentor's role is to help the product manager grow, not just by providing insights but by checking in on progress and offering advice on overcoming challenges. The beauty of a mentor is that they offer accountability with a long-term view,

focused on the product manager's career trajectory and personal development.

- **Team Members:** Within a product development team, accountability doesn't just flow downward from supervisors; it's also a horizontal relationship between team members. Product managers often work closely with engineers, designers, and marketers, and they rely on each other to meet deadlines, provide feedback, and collaborate on problem-solving. In fact, agile methodologies like Scrum and Kanban, which are common in product management, emphasize team-based accountability. Daily stand-up meetings, sprint reviews, and retrospectives are all designed to foster transparency and accountability among team members.
- **Customers or Users:** Believe it or not, customers or users can serve as accountability partners too. In many ways, the product manager is accountable to the users who rely on the product. Customer feedback, reviews, and engagement metrics hold product managers accountable for delivering a high-quality experience. In some cases, especially with B2B products, key clients may be directly involved in product development, offering feedback and expecting the product manager to meet specific milestones or deliverables.

The Benefits of Accountability in Product Management

There's plenty of evidence that accountability drives results, especially in professional settings. A study by the American

Society of Training and Development (ASTD) found that individuals are 65% more likely to meet their goals when they have an accountability partner. And, if they have a specific accountability meeting with that person, their chances of success increase to 95%. Imagine how this applies in product management, where deadlines are critical and projects can span months or even years.

Additionally, Harvard Business Review reported that team members who share accountability experience higher levels of engagement, collaboration, and trust. These factors directly impact the quality of work and overall team morale, which are essential in managing complex product development cycles.

Accountability Partners in Life: Who Holds You Accountable?

Just as accountability partners are crucial in product management, they're equally valuable in your personal life. Whether you're trying to hit the gym, learn a new skill, or spend more time with your family, having someone to hold you accountable can significantly boost your chances of success. But who fills this role in your personal life?

- **Friends or Family:** Friends and family are the most common accountability partners in personal life. They know you best, and if they care about you, they won't hesitate to call you out when you start slacking on your goals. Whether it's a friend who joins you for a workout or a sibling who checks in on your progress, these close relationships create a natural framework for accountability.

- **Colleagues or Peers:** For personal or professional development goals, colleagues or peers can be great accountability partners. If you're working on a skill, like public speaking or coding, a coworker who's pursuing the same goal can help you stay on track. You can check in with each other, share progress, and even offer constructive feedback.
- **Coaches or Mentors:** In life, much like in business, mentors can provide a broader sense of accountability. If you're working with a life coach or a career mentor, they will help you define your goals, track your progress, and challenge you to push through obstacles. These relationships tend to focus more on long-term growth and development, making them perfect for people who need guidance in multiple areas of life.

The Science Behind Accountability

If you're thinking, "Yeah, accountability partners sound great, but do they really make that much of a difference?" The answer is a resounding yes. Research has consistently shown that accountability increases the likelihood of goal achievement. In addition to the ASTD study mentioned earlier, there's evidence from behavioral psychology that supports the idea of "public commitment."

In one study, participants who publicly committed to a goal were far more likely to follow through than those who kept their goals private. Why? Because the fear of disappointing others creates a psychological drive to maintain your commitment. This effect is often referred to as "social accountability," and it's one of the reasons why having someone check in on you can significantly boost your success rate.

Another study from the Dominican University found that people who shared their goals and had an accountability partner were 33% more likely to achieve their objectives compared to those who went at it alone . In personal life and professional settings, this concept holds true: being accountable to someone else makes it much harder to slack off, procrastinate, or abandon a goal.

Setting Up Effective Accountability Relationships

Having an accountability partner isn't just about finding someone who will check in on you occasionally. It requires a structured approach to ensure you both get the most out of the relationship. Here are some tips for making it work:

- **Define the Goal:** Make sure both you and your accountability partner are clear on what you're trying to achieve. Whether it's a product milestone or a personal fitness goal, clarity is key.
- **Set Check-In Points:** Don't just rely on vague promises to "keep each other in the loop." Set specific times to check in, whether it's weekly or bi-weekly, to ensure regular progress updates.
- **Offer Constructive Feedback:** Accountability isn't about criticizing every misstep—it's about providing constructive feedback to help the other person improve. Keep the tone supportive but honest.
- **Celebrate Wins:** Don't forget to celebrate milestones and accomplishments. This not only boosts morale

but reinforces the behavior of working toward the goal.

Reflection and Actionable Advice:

- **Identify an Accountability Partner:** Whether for work or life, find someone who will help you stay committed to your goals. This could be a mentor, friend, or even a colleague working toward a similar objective.
- **Set Clear Expectations:** Define what success looks like, how often you'll check in, and what kind of support or feedback you expect from each other.
- **Stay Consistent:** Check in regularly, share your progress, and don't shy away from difficult conversations if you're falling behind. The point of having an accountability partner is to push through the hard times, not just to high-five each other when things are going well.

Another way to set goals, track progress, and assess whether it's time to pivot is through the product management concept of gamification.

Using Gamification

Let's face it—product management and personal development can sometimes feel like a chore. In product management, gamification is used to boost user engagement and retention by making experiences more enjoyable. If you've ever found yourself obsessed with tracking your daily steps or binge-playing an app because you wanted to unlock the next level, you've experienced gamification in action.

Here are a few ways product managers incorporate gamification into their strategies:

- **Points, Badges, and Leaderboards:** Many apps offer users points or badges for completing certain actions. Whether it's reaching a new milestone, sharing content, or achieving a fitness goal, users are rewarded for engaging with the product. Leaderboards, in turn, create a sense of competition, pushing users to outdo themselves (or others).
- **Challenges and Rewards:** Product managers often create challenges that encourage users to stay active on the platform. For example, fitness apps may create thirty-day challenges, rewarding users for sticking to their workout routines. These short-term goals, paired with rewards like unlocking new features or receiving discounts, keep users engaged.
- **Progress Bars and Feedback Loops:** A simple progress bar can be surprisingly motivating. Seeing your progress visually, whether in the form of a bar or a percentage, taps into the brain's desire to complete tasks. Product managers use these visual cues to encourage users to finish what they've started, whether that's filling out a profile, completing a course, or reaching the next stage in a program.

Gamification works because it taps into intrinsic motivators —like the desire for achievement, competition, and mastery. And it turns otherwise mundane tasks into opportunities for growth and rewards. But what if we applied those same principles to our own personal growth?

Whether it's sticking to a workout routine, learning a new skill, or meeting those never-ending deadlines, staying motivated over the long haul is tough. At its core, **gamification** is the process of adding game-like elements—points, challenges, rewards, and competition—to non-game contexts, like personal growth to make it more engaging and rewarding. It's like turning your to-do list into a video game, only instead of leveling up in a fictional world, you're leveling up in real life.

So how can you use gamification in your personal life? Think about the areas where you want to improve—whether it's exercising regularly, learning a new skill, or being more productive—and find ways to make the process more fun and engaging. Here are a few examples:

- **Create Your Own Point System:** Reward yourself for completing tasks by assigning points to your activities. Maybe you give yourself 10 points for every workout or 5 points for reading a new book. Once you reach a certain number of points, reward yourself with something you enjoy—whether it's a small treat, a day off, or a fun activity you've been putting off. It's all about turning personal growth into a game.
- **Use Progress Tracking Apps:** Apps like Duolingo and Habitica use gamification to help you stay on track with learning or developing new habits. You earn points and rewards for completing tasks, and some apps even let you level up or unlock new features as you make progress.

- **Set Challenges and Compete:** Create challenges for yourself and, if possible, involve friends or family. Whether it's a step challenge, a reading goal, or a productivity streak, adding a competitive element can increase your motivation to stick with it. And remember, the rewards can be anything that makes you feel accomplished, from unlocking a cheat day to taking a well-deserved break.

The beauty of gamification is that it turns your goals into something fun and engaging, making it easier to stay motivated and track your progress.

Reflection and Actionable Advice:

- **Set up your own point or reward system** for your personal goals. Identify tasks that are important to you and assign points or rewards to them.
- **Join or create challenges** in areas where you want to grow. Involving others adds a fun, competitive element to your personal development.
- **Track your progress visually**—whether through apps, charts, or simple checklists. Seeing your progress will give you that little dopamine hit you need to keep going.

Gamification turns goal setting into an engaging, fun process —because personal growth doesn't always have to be so serious!

Now, if you are more analytical, gamification may not be the right strategy for you. You might be more of a data analytics type and what to track progress in more serious ways. No worries!

Tracking Progress Through Behavioral Data Analytics

Data is the backbone of any successful product, and the same can be said for your personal development. In product management, **behavioral data analytics** is used to track user behavior, measure engagement, and predict future trends. Essentially, it's about collecting and analyzing data to see what's working, what's not, and what changes need to be made to optimize a product's performance.

But here's the thing—**you** are a product too. And if product managers can use behavioral data to improve their products, why can't you do the same for your personal goals? Tracking your own behaviors and habits through data can give you valuable insights into what's helping you grow, what's holding you back, and where you can make improvements.

So, let's explore this concept as used in product management and then (you guessed it) apply it to you as a product!

Behavioral Data Analytics in Product Management

In the world of product management, tracking and analyzing user behavior is crucial for creating a product that people love. Here are a few key areas where behavioral data analytics comes into play:

- **User Retention and Engagement:** Product managers track how often users return to the app, how long they stay, and what features they interact with the most. This data helps them understand what keeps users engaged and what drives them away. If users stop engaging with a certain feature, it's a sign that something needs to be adjusted or improved.

- **A/B Testing and Iteration:** Product teams often use A/B testing to compare two versions of a feature, interface, or marketing campaign. They track how users interact with each version and then use the data to choose the most successful approach. It's all about collecting data, analyzing it, and iterating to optimize the user experience.
- **Personalization and Predictive Analytics:** Behavioral data allows product managers to tailor the user experience. By tracking user preferences and behaviors, they can offer personalized recommendations, predict future actions, and create a more customized experience. Think about how Netflix recommends shows based on what you've watched—that's behavioral data analytics at work.

In short, data analytics helps product managers make informed decisions that lead to better user experiences and ultimately, more successful products.

So how does this translate to your personal life?

Behavioral Data Analytics in Personal Development

Just like product managers track data to improve their products, you can track your own behaviors and habits to improve your personal growth. Here's how:

- **Track Your Habits and Routines:** Start by tracking the habits and behaviors you want to improve. You can use apps like Strides, HabitBull, or even a simple spreadsheet to log your activities. Whether it's tracking your workouts, your diet, or how much time you spend on social media, the key is collecting data on the behaviors that impact your goals.
- **Analyze Your Patterns:** Once you've gathered some data, take a look at the patterns. Do you tend to skip your workout when you stay up late? Are there certain days when you're more productive? Analyzing your data can reveal valuable insights about your habits, helping you make more informed decisions moving forward.
- **Use Data to Make Adjustments:** Once you understand your behavior patterns, use that information to adjust your routine. If you notice that you're more productive in the morning, for example, you might shift your most important tasks to earlier in the day. Or, if your data shows that you tend to snack more in the afternoon, you can plan to have healthier options on hand. It's about using your own data to optimize your habits for personal growth.
- **Measure Progress and Celebrate Wins:** Behavioral data isn't just about identifying problems—it's also about celebrating progress. Use your data to track your improvements over time, and reward yourself when you hit milestones. Just as product managers track user engagement to measure success, you can track your habits to see how far you've come.

Reflection and Actionable Advice:

- **Start tracking your habits and behaviors** in the areas where you want to grow. You can use an app, a journal, or even a spreadsheet.
- **Look for patterns in your data**—both positive and negative. What are you doing well? Where can you improve? Use this information to make informed changes to your routine.
- **Iterate based on your data.** Just like a product manager uses data to improve a product, you can use your own data to fine-tune your habits and routines for better results.

By applying behavioral data analytics to your personal growth, you can make more informed decisions, track your progress, and celebrate your successes along the way. After all, what gets measured, gets managed.

Finally, when it comes to setting goals and measuring success, we cannot skip past the little wins along the way.

Celebrating Success: The Importance of Milestones

In product management, celebrating success along the way is more than just throwing a party—although those can be fun too. It's about recognizing progress, reflecting on what's been achieved, and using that momentum to push forward. Product managers often celebrate key wins such as successful product launches, the completion of important development phases, or meeting key performance indicators (KPIs). These celebrations aren't just for fun; they serve as critical checkpoints to boost team morale, recognize hard work, and align the team around the next set of objectives.

Product managers typically celebrate milestones in a variety of ways, including:

- **Public Recognition:** Product managers often give shout-outs to individuals or teams who made significant contributions during meetings or through internal communications. This could be a dedicated "win" announcement during all-hands meetings, or recognition emails that call out specific efforts.
- **Small Celebrations:** Many teams mark smaller wins with casual celebrations like a team lunch, virtual happy hour (in today's remote world), or even a fun group activity. This is a way to pause and recognize the work done before moving on to the next stage.
- **Gamification Elements:** Some teams use gamification to make goal tracking and milestone celebrations fun. For example, they might use a point system where team members earn rewards for meeting objectives or solving key problems, such as earning badges or rewards.
- **Celebrating Product Launches:** A successful product launch is often celebrated with more significant activities, like launch parties, swag for the team, or even performance bonuses. These bigger milestones help everyone feel part of the product's journey and success.

The Science of Celebrating Milestones

Research shows that recognizing achievements—whether big or small—has a measurable impact on motivation and morale. Celebrating milestones along the way to a larger goal can improve long-term performance, increase engagement, and even lead to better decision-making. A study conducted by Harvard Business Review found that tracking small achievements and celebrating them creates an "inner work life" for employees that boosts overall job satisfaction and productivity (Amabile & Kramer, 2011).

Here's why celebrating milestones is so powerful:

- **Boosts Motivation:** A 2018 study published in Organizational Behavior and Human Decision Processes found that employees who celebrated small wins were more motivated to keep working toward larger goals (Anseel, et al., 2018). These mini-celebrations create dopamine releases in the brain, reinforcing positive behavior and making team members more eager to achieve the next goal.
- **Builds Team Cohesion:** Recognizing accomplishments fosters a sense of community and collective achievement, especially in team settings. **Forbes** reports that celebrating wins publicly strengthens relationships between team members and encourages collaboration (Zenger, 2018).
- **Enhances Mental Well-Being:** Celebrating success helps reduce burnout and boosts mental well-being by reinforcing the notion that hard work is being recognized and valued. A 2019 study in the Journal of Applied Psychology showed that when employees felt

recognized, they were more likely to report higher levels of job satisfaction and lower levels of stress (Allen, et al., 2019).
- **Creates Positive Feedback Loops:** By celebrating successes, product managers create positive feedback loops where team members feel appreciated and are more likely to engage deeply in future projects. This has the dual benefit of retaining talent and fostering innovation within teams.

The principle of celebrating milestones applies equally to personal growth. In life, you might celebrate reaching a savings target, or even finishing a major project. It's not just about crossing the finish line but about taking a moment to appreciate the journey. Here's how you can apply this concept in your own life:

- **Reward Yourself for Small Wins:** If you've been working toward a health goal, like exercising regularly, don't wait until you reach your end goal to celebrate. After each week of hitting your exercise targets, treat yourself to something small that brings you joy—maybe a healthy snack, a relaxing evening off, or buying a new book you've been eyeing.
- **Publicly Acknowledge Your Progress:** Sharing your wins with others makes them feel more real. Just as a product manager recognizes a team's progress, you can celebrate by telling a friend or family member about your achievement. This not only helps you stay accountable but also gives you a boost of external encouragement.

- **Mark Big Milestones with Something Special:** For larger milestones, plan bigger rewards. Maybe you book a weekend getaway when you reach a financial goal or treat yourself to something special when you hit a personal growth target. These celebrations serve as a reminder of your hard work and give you something to look forward to during the tough times.

Reflection and Actionable Advice:

- **Set mini-milestones:** Break your larger goals into smaller, more manageable chunks, and celebrate when you reach each one. This keeps motivation high and helps avoid burnout.
- **Incorporate gamification:** Whether you're managing a team or setting personal goals, consider using gamification to make tracking progress and celebrating success more engaging.
- **Be mindful of team dynamics:** If you're in a leadership role, make sure your celebrations acknowledge all contributions. Publicly thanking team members can enhance morale and foster team cohesion.
- **Celebrate without overdoing it:** While celebrating milestones is essential, balance it with focus. Too many celebrations can create a "victory high" that distracts from ongoing work.

Celebrating success is an essential component of both product management and personal growth. It fosters motivation, strengthens teams, and creates a sense of accomplishment that fuels continued progress. By acknowledging the milestones along your journey—whether in a project or in life—you maintain the energy and drive necessary to achieve your long-term goals.

Of course, at this point you might be thinking this is great information and all but how do I put it all together—

I'm glad you asked—you build a roadmap!

Chapter 7
Crafting Your Roadmap

In product management, the roadmap is a high-level plan that outlines a product's development, key milestones, and long-term goals. It's not set in stone (speed limits and route might vary), but it gives everyone a clear direction, ensuring the product grows and adapts while staying true to its purpose. Your life, too, benefits from this approach—a flexible yet focused roadmap helps you break down big, often overwhelming life goals into achievable phases.

Now, this is where the rubber meets the road so to speak (pun intended). Much like a product's lifecycle—introduction, growth, maturity, and possible reinvention—your life can be organized into similar phases (sound familiar). Here's a quick review of the phases:

- **Introduction Phase (The Launch):** This is your early adulthood or any time you're diving into something new—a new career, a new relationship, or even a hobby. Just like in product management, this is the time to experiment, gather feedback, and make adjustments.

- **Growth Phase (The Hustle):** This is when you've found your stride, and now it's all about building momentum. In your career, this might be the time to seek promotions or expand your expertise. In personal life, it might involve building deeper relationships or mastering new skills. During this phase, you're working hard to establish yourself, just as a product gains market share.
- **Maturity Phase (The Plateau):** The maturity phase is where things stabilize. You've achieved a level of success or comfort, but the danger here is stagnation. It's important to continue innovating and finding new ways to stay fulfilled. This might mean shifting focus, mentoring others, or exploring new personal interests.
- **Reinvention (The Pivot):** At some point, you'll hit a point where the old ways just don't work anymore. Whether you're switching careers, picking up new skills, or deciding to change your lifestyle, this phase is all about embracing reinvention. Product managers love this part—it's all about keeping things fresh, exciting, and aligned with your evolving needs.

By breaking your project, product life cycle or—life—into these phases, you can better manage your expectations and goals. Just like a product roadmap, your life roadmap is a living document that should be revisited and adjusted as your circumstances change. And let's face it, life loves throwing curveballs—so flexibility is key. So, let's break down the roadmap for both production management and how it can be applied to life.

Product Management Roadmaps

In product management, a roadmap provides a strategic outline of the product's goals, milestones, and deliverables over a specific time frame. Here are a couple of common examples:

1. **Feature-Based Roadmap**
   - **Goal:** Add new features to enhance user experience or increase market competitiveness.
   - **Time Frame:** Twelve months.

Example:

1. **Q1:** User feedback analysis, defining feature set, prototyping.
2. **Q2:** Feature development, internal testing, early user feedback.
3. **Q3:** Beta launch of features, bug fixes, user onboarding materials.
4. **Q4:** Official launch, marketing campaigns, post-launch user feedback.
5. **Goal-Oriented Roadmap**
   - **Goal:** Achieve specific business outcomes (e.g., increase user engagement, boost revenue).
   - **Time Frame:** Six to twelve months.

Example:
- **Goal 1:** Increase daily active users (DAU) by 20 percent.

- **Q1:** User research, implementing user engagement features.
- **Q2:** Launch engagement features, monitor user data.
- **Q3:** Optimize features based on feedback, scale marketing efforts.

- **Goal 2:** Boost annual recurring revenue (ARR) by 15 percent.

- **Q1:** Identify new markets, develop freemium models.
- **Q2:** Launch freemium models, initiate marketing campaigns.
- **Q3:** Monitor conversions, optimize pricing strategy.

Fairly simple, right? But what would a life roadmap look like you ask. Well, it may not be as clearly defined as a product management roadmap because—well—life. There are more twists and turns out in the wild than in a more controlled environment. However, it is still possible to line out long and short-term roadmaps in life.

Creating a Life Roadmap Template

A **life roadmap** helps you break down your long-term vision into manageable phases, ensuring that your personal and professional goals are strategically aligned. You want to focus on:

- **Long-Term Vision:** (Write your long-term vision or life goal, such as "build a fulfilling career while maintaining strong personal relationships and pursuing personal passions.")

- **Core Values:** (List your core values that guide your decisions, such as "integrity, creativity, resilience.")

With these two areas defined, you can lay out the roadmap on how to get there in phases.

Phase 1: Exploration and Early Development (Introduction Phase)

Time Frame: (E.g., Ages 20-30 or Next 5 Years)

- **Key Goals:**
  - Explore career opportunities and personal interests.
  - Build foundational skills in [specific field].
  - Strengthen personal and professional relationships.
- **Milestones:**
  - Complete a degree or certification in [field].
  - Land first job or internship in desired industry.
  - Develop a strong network of mentors and peers.
  - Set up a personal health and wellness routine.
- **Action Steps:**
  - Attend industry conferences and networking events.
  - Take on side projects or hobbies to explore personal interests.
  - Set up regular check-ins with mentors for feedback.
  - Begin budgeting and saving for the future.

. . .

Phase 2: Growth and Career Building (Growth Phase)

Time Frame: E.g., Ages 30-40 or Next 5-10 Years)

- **Key Goals:**
    - Achieve professional success and recognition in [career field].
    - Develop leadership skills and take on larger responsibilities.
    - Establish personal routines that promote long-term well-being.
- **Milestones:**
    - Earn a promotion or transition into a more senior role.
    - Begin public speaking, mentoring, or teaching in your field.
    - Start a side hustle or passion project.
    - Invest in long-term financial goals (e.g., home purchase, retirement savings).
- **Action Steps:**
    - Continue upskilling through courses and certifications.
    - Mentor junior colleagues or students in your field.
    - Refine personal routines (e.g., fitness, mindfulness practices).
    - Set up an investment plan for retirement.

Phase 3: Sustaining Success and Personal Fulfillment (Maturity Phase)

Time Frame: (E.g., Ages 40-55 or Next 10 Years)

- **Key Goals:**
  - Maintain and grow professional success.
  - Prioritize personal fulfillment and work-life balance.
  - Develop a legacy or long-term impact through work or community involvement.
- **Milestones:**
  - Achieve executive or thought leader status in your industry.
  - Shift focus to mentoring and developing the next generation.
  - Travel or engage in life experiences that align with personal interests.
  - Focus on family, relationships, and personal satisfaction.
- **Action Steps:**
  - Build a succession plan at work or in your business.
  - Write a book, start a podcast, or share your expertise with a wider audience.
  - Volunteer or take on pro-bono work that reflects your passions.
  - Create time for personal hobbies and interests outside of work.

Phase 4: Reinvention and Renewal (Reinvention Phase)

Time Frame: (E.g., Ages 55+ or Next 10-20 Years)

- **Key Goals:**
  - Redefine personal and professional goals based on new opportunities onal growth, family, and community impact.
  - Shift towards legacy building, exploring new passions, or pivoting into new fields.
- **Milestones:**
  - Transition to consulting, advisory roles, or new ventures.
  - Cultivate deep personal relationships and community involvement.
  - Focus on health and well-being for long-term vitality.
  - Develop and execute a legacy project (e.g., charitable work, community impact).
- **Action Steps:**
  - Plan for semi-retirement or a career pivot.
  - Focus on self-care and health to ensure long-term well-being.
  - Engage in creative pursuits or projects that bring joy.
  - Plan for financial security and estate planning.

Whew! If you've broken down the phases, set your milestones, and outlined your action steps, you are ahead of probably everyone else—over achiever. You're like the navigator of a grand adventure, complete with treasure maps (minus the pirates, hopefully). But remember, even the most well-thought-out plans need regular pit stops. Life is unpredictable—a scenic detour here, an unexpected roadblock there—and it's in these moments that reflection becomes your best friend. Consider the following to keep your sanity in the chaos:

- **Quarterly Check-Ins:** Treat these like mini pit stops on your journey. Are you still on track, or did you take a wrong turn into Procrastination Town? Adjust your roadmap as life unfolds. Flexibility is key. After all, no one likes a GPS that refuses to recalculate.
- **Annual Goal Review:** Think of this as your yearly tune-up. Check your progress, celebrate the small victories (yes, finishing that one long-put-off project does count), and tweak your roadmap to better align with new priorities.
- **Celebrate Successes:** Speaking of which—don't forget to throw a mini party for your milestones! Maybe not a full-blown parade, but definitely give yourself a pat on the back. Whether you've crushed a major career goal or just managed to keep your plants alive for an entire year, it all counts.

In the end, roadmaps are about direction, not perfection. Sure, you'll hit some bumps along the way, but those bumps add character (and maybe a funny story or two). The important thing is that you're moving forward with intention, equipped with the tools you need to navigate life's twists and turns.

Reflection and Actionable Advice:

Crafting a life roadmap isn't just about setting goals—it's

about breaking down those goals into manageable steps and staying flexible enough to adapt along the way.

- Look at your current life roadmap. Are there areas where you've been stuck? Could the obstacle be a lack of clear steps, or is it more about fear of making the wrong choice?
- Pick one area of your life where you've been hesitant to make progress. Break it down into smaller, bite-sized actions that you can start on immediately.
- Set a micro-goal for the week. For example, if you've been meaning to network more, commit to attending one event or reaching out to one new person. Celebrate the small milestones as you achieve them.

Now, if you're ready, it's time to zoom out a bit. Because here's the thing—no matter how meticulously you plan, life doesn't happen in isolation. Every decision you make ripples out and connects to something bigger. This is where systems thinking comes in.

Think of it like this: if your life roadmap is the detailed itinerary for your journey, then systems thinking is like understanding the entire ecosystem you're traveling through—the weather patterns, the road conditions, the other travelers. It's about anticipating how the various elements of your life interact, ensuring that you're not just driving blindfolded through a maze of unintended consequences.

Ready to expand your vision? Let's dive into systems thinking and start seeing the forest and the trees.

Systems Thinking: Seeing the Forest and the Trees

Systems thinking is the product manager's crystal ball—it's all about looking beyond the immediate and obvious to anticipate the ripple effects of your decisions. Imagine you're a product manager deciding to introduce a new feature. You know it will impact more than just the product—it might change user behavior, require new marketing strategies, and even influence future development. Life works the same way. Every decision you make doesn't exist in a vacuum; it has a broader impact on other parts of your life.

Look at it this way—you've got your roadmap, and you're cruising along, feeling like you've got this whole "life management" thing figured out. But then—BAM!—life throws a curveball. Suddenly, that promotion you were gunning for means more late nights at the office, and your dreams of work-life balance start to look more like work with occasional naps. This is where systems thinking comes in to save the day.

If life is a giant puzzle, systems thinking is the tool that helps you see how all the pieces fit together. It's like stepping back from a jigsaw puzzle you've been working on for hours only to realize you've been trying to cram a sky piece into a corner meant for trees. In other words, it helps you understand the connections between the small decisions you make and the big picture they affect.

So, you've got the analogy but let's take a hard look at systems thinking connections.

. . .

What is Systems Thinking, Anyway?

Systems thinking is about recognizing that everything is connected. It's like the butterfly effect but without the dramatic time travel plotlines. In product management, it means thinking beyond today's to-do list and considering how adding a new feature could change user behavior, impact the budget, or even make future development trickier. In life, it's realizing that your decision to binge-watch an entire series over the weekend might impact your ability to function like a normal human being come Monday.

Systems thinking has a few key components for avoiding life's chain reactions. They are:

- **Interconnectedness:** In systems thinking, everything you do is part of a larger web. It's like playing Jenga—sure, pulling one block out might seem harmless, but eventually, the whole thing could come crashing down if you're not careful. In product management, that's the equivalent of rolling out a shiny new feature without thinking about how it'll interact with the rest of the product. In life, it's deciding to take on a side hustle without considering how it'll eat into your Netflix time (and, you know, your sleep).
- **Feedback Loops:** Systems thinking is all about those feedback loops—where your actions either reinforce or counteract themselves over time. For example, you decide to eat healthy, and after a week of salads, you feel great. That's a **positive feedback loop:** doing something good makes you feel good, so you keep

doing it. But then there's the **negative feedback loop:** like when you ignore the dishes piling up in your sink, and suddenly, you're out of clean forks. Now you're forced to eat cereal with a ladle, and you promise yourself to wash dishes before they hit critical mass. Feedback loops help you adjust course before things spiral out of control—whether it's your health, your work, or your ever-growing laundry pile.

- **Emergent Properties:** Here's where things get wild. Sometimes, when all the pieces of a system work together, they create something bigger than the sum of their parts. It's like when you throw together some dough, sauce, and cheese and suddenly—BAM!—you've got pizza. In product management, emergent properties could be the result of combining two features that work so well together, users can't live without them. In life, it's how balancing work, health, and relationships can lead to a deep sense of fulfilment—something greater than the parts individually would have achieved.
- Systems thinking in the wild can take many forms. However, there are some key questions that are fairly consistent. In product management, you may decide to add a cool new feature to your app. Awesome, right? But wait—before you high-five the dev team, Systems Thinking asks:
    - How does this new feature affect user experience?
    - Will it cause more bugs or slow things down?
    - Are there any hidden costs or dependencies? Like when you decide to adopt a pet and forget that "puppy eyes" come with chewed-up shoes and 5

a.m. walks—Systems Thinking stops you from overlooking the big picture.

Now, let's apply this to real life. You decide to take up a new hobby—say, learning to play the guitar. But Systems Thinking says, "Hold up!" Sure, it sounds fun now, but—

- Will you have time to practice?
- What if it cuts into your time for family, friends, or (gasp) your nap schedule?

In systems thinking, you're forced to zoom out and see how adding one thing impacts everything else. The guitar might turn out to be your new best friend—or just an expensive dust collector.

Or, let's say you decide to take on a new job with a higher salary but longer hours. At first glance, it seems like a win—you're getting paid more, and your career is advancing. But systems thinking asks you to look at the bigger picture:

- Will those longer hours affect your health? Your relationships?
- Will you have less time to pursue personal interests or self-care?

These are the kinds of long-term impacts that systems thinking encourages you to anticipate.

In life, systems thinking helps you:

- **Avoid unintended consequences:** By understanding how your actions influence different areas of your life, you can make more informed choices and minimize potential negative outcomes.
- **Optimize decision-making:** When you consider the long-term impact of your decisions, you can align your actions with your ultimate goals and values, ensuring that you're not just solving today's problems but setting yourself up for future success.
- **Embrace interconnectedness:** Systems thinking helps you appreciate the interconnectedness of your personal and professional life. A decision that improves one area often has a ripple effect on others.

Of course, these are two small examples and looking around the corners can lead you down rabbit holes you never knew existed. So, how can you become a systems thinker without getting overwhelmed? Consider the following:

- **Zoom Out (Like, Way Out):** Before making any major decision, zoom out like you're trying to see the whole forest, not just the individual trees. Ask yourself: How will this decision affect not just the immediate goal, but everything else around it? Think of it like planning a dinner party—you don't just make the main course and forget about drinks, sides, or seating. Systems Thinking means considering how every element interacts with the others.

- **Pay Attention to Feedback Loops:** Ever start a workout routine and suddenly feel more energized, so you stick with it? That's a positive feedback loop. Or maybe you've stayed up too late scrolling on your phone and now you're tired, so you grab an extra cup of coffee... only to end up wired and unable to sleep again. Negative loop. In product management, feedback loops show up when user behavior starts reinforcing or countering the effects of new features. In life, look for those loops that either push you forward or pull you back.
- **Think Long-Term**: Systems Thinking forces you to play the long game. It's tempting to make decisions based on short-term gains, but doing so can lead to long-term headaches. Spending money on enjoyment and fun might feel like a win today, but what if it comes with a health condition that isn't covered in your insurance? Systems Thinking says: Let's look at this move two, five, ten years down the road. Will this still be a good decision when the initial excitement wears off?
- **Accept the Trade-Offs:** Here's the thing: Every decision comes with trade-offs. Systems Thinking isn't about avoiding them but accepting them with open eyes. Want that promotion? It might mean sacrificing some personal time. Thinking about starting a business? Be prepared for the hustle. Systems Thinking helps you decide what you're willing to give up for what you want most. Kind of like choosing between watching just one more episode of your favorite show and getting enough

sleep for work tomorrow. Spoiler: Sleep always wins in the long run.

Systems thinking is a critical process when seeking success in product management or life. In product management, skipping systems thinking is like launching a feature without considering how it affects the user experience or backend infrastructure. It might work for a minute, but soon, everything's on fire. In life, skipping systems thinking is like saying "yes" to every opportunity without considering how you'll fit it all in. It's all fun and games until you're double-booked, sleep-deprived, and wondering why you agreed to join three different committees. Oops.

So, what have we learned?

Systems thinking is your cheat code for seeing the big picture—both in product management and life. It's what stops you from making impulsive decisions that might make you happy now but drive you nuts later. Sure, it's a little extra effort upfront, but it's way better than dealing with unintended consequences down the road. Plus, it helps you turn life's curveballs into strategic plays.

Now, with systems thinking in your toolkit, you're ready to level up. But don't get too comfortable—as we will dive into frugal innovation—because sometimes, you've got to work smarter, not harder, to make the most of what you've got.

Frugal Innovation: Making the Most of Limited Resources

If you've ever tried to make a gourmet meal from what's left in your fridge on a Sunday night—half a tomato, some wilted spinach, and a block of mystery cheese—you've already dabbled in frugal innovation. In product management, frugal innovation is about creating valuable products using limited resources. It's the art of being scrappy without sacrificing quality—like making a fancy app with just a small team or launching a product on a shoestring budget.

In life, it's the same deal. Frugal innovation is the key to figuring out how to achieve big goals without an unlimited supply of time, money, or energy. It's all about leveraging what you've got and making it work. Think MacGyvering your way through life—solving problems with duct tape and chewing gum (metaphorically, of course). Whether it's finding ways to save money while traveling the world or learning how to hustle between multiple jobs, frugal innovation is your survival toolkit for the modern world.

In product management, companies like Tata Motors are famous for frugal innovation. When they developed the Tata Nano—marketed as the world's most affordable car—they had to rethink traditional car manufacturing to strip out unnecessary costs while still delivering a vehicle that worked. No leather seats or fancy GPS, but hey, it got you from A to B!

Another classic example of frugal innovation in product management is the rise of Jugaad innovation in India, where companies have developed low-cost solutions to meet the needs of resource-constrained markets. For instance, instead of developing high-end medical devices, companies have innovated with cost-effective alternatives that deliver the same results. In life, this mindset can help you find creative solutions when you're low on time, money, or energy—whether that's upcycling old furniture or starting a business from your kitchen table.

Frugal innovation might look like:

- **Repurposing existing features:** Instead of building a new feature from scratch, product managers often find ways to adapt or extend what's already there to meet new user needs.
- **Leveraging low-cost tools and solutions:** Rather than investing in expensive software or hardware, they might use more affordable options that get the job done without blowing the budget.
- **Maximizing team productivity:** By focusing on the most impactful tasks and avoiding unnecessary busywork, product managers can get more done with limited resources.

In life, frugal innovation might look like transforming that side hustle into your main gig without taking on huge debt. It's about doing more with less and figuring out how to use your resources (however limited) to create something valuable. Got just fifteen minutes between meetings? Use it to meditate, journal, or work on a new skill. As they say, time is money—especially when you're short on both! Frugal innovation includes:

- **Time management:** Don't have hours to dedicate to a

side project? Try breaking it into small, manageable chunks and work on it a little each day.
- **Financial planning:** Instead of spending a fortune on the latest tech gadget, find budget-friendly alternatives or make do with what you already have.
- **Personal energy:** Prioritize what matters most to you and let go of activities or commitments that don't add value to your life. You only have so much time and energy, so spend it wisely.

Reflection and Actionable Advice:

Frugal innovation isn't about deprivation; it's about making the most of what you have. Whether you're managing a tight budget or limited time, it's all about resourcefulness.

- Think about an area in your life where you've been waiting for "the right time" or "enough resources" to make progress. Could you take a frugal innovation approach and start now with what you already have?
- Identify one specific goal in your life and apply the frugal innovation mindset. How can you accomplish this goal with the resources you currently have?
- Focus on small wins—find ways to reduce costs, streamline tasks, or repurpose resources. For example, if you want to start a side project but don't have funding, can you leverage free tools or barter skills with friends?

So, you've mastered frugal innovation and learned how to squeeze every last drop of value out of your resources. But here's the thing—no matter how scrappy or creative you are, there's a limit to what you can do solo. That's where platform thinking comes in. If frugal innovation is about doing more with less, then platform thinking is about doing more by tapping into an ecosystem. It's like being a superhero with a sidekick—sure, you can save the day on your own, but it's a lot easier (and more fun) when you've got a whole team behind you.

Leveraging Platform Thinking: Building Your Ecosystem

So now that you've learned how to make magic out of thin air with frugal innovation, let's talk about platform thinking—because even the scrappiest innovator needs a solid network.

Platform thinking is like building a village around your product or life. In the business world, it's the concept behind platforms like Amazon or Uber—creating an ecosystem where various users and services interact and exchange value. Rather than just focusing on one product, platform thinking considers how all the parts work together to create a network that's greater than the sum of its parts. It's all about creating an ecosystem that connects different users, tools, and resources to deliver value. In product management, platform thinking allows companies to scale and innovate by building networks that grow organically.

Apple's App Store is a classic example of platform thinking. Instead of just making iPhones, Apple built a platform that allows developers to create apps, which in turn makes the iPhone more valuable to consumers. It's a win-win for everyone involved—the developers, Apple, and the users.

. . .

In Product Management, Platform Thinking Looks Like:

- **Creating ecosystems of value:** By connecting users, developers, and third-party providers, product managers can create platforms that grow through the contributions of others (think the App Store or Google Play).
- **Leveraging partnerships:** Successful platforms often involve partnerships with other companies or developers, allowing them to offer more value to their users without having to build everything in-house.
- **Fostering user collaboration:** Platforms thrive when users contribute content, services, or reviews, creating a self-sustaining ecosystem.

But here's the thing—platform thinking isn't just for business. You can apply the same concept to your personal and professional life by building your own "platform," or network, of people, skills, and resources that support your growth.

In life, platform thinking is about creating and maintaining relationships, resources, and opportunities that build each other up. It's like your network on steroids. Instead of seeing your friends, family, coworkers, and mentors as separate entities, platform thinking recognizes how they can all connect to help you achieve your goals (and vice versa). Your mentor gives you career advice, which you then share with your peer, who invites you to a networking event where you meet your next collaborator. See how it all ties together? It's like hosting a potluck where everyone brings a dish and, before you know it, you've got a five-course meal.

In Life, Platform Thinking Looks Like:

- **Building a personal network:** Just like platforms connect users, you can build a network of people who help you grow. This might include mentors, colleagues, friends, and family. Each person adds value to your life in different ways.
- **Creating reciprocal relationships:** Think of your network as a two-way street. Just as platforms thrive on user input, your relationships flourish when both sides give and receive value. Offer support, guidance, and connections, and you'll find that others do the same for you.
- **Leveraging resources:** Just as platforms leverage external developers and partners, you can use the resources around you to achieve your goals. This might mean using free online courses to learn a new skill or tapping into a community of like-minded individuals for support and advice.

A real-life example of platform thinking could be building a personal brand on social media or LinkedIn. By engaging with other professionals, sharing your expertise, and contributing to discussions, you're creating a platform where your personal and professional network can grow organically. Over time, this platform becomes an invaluable resource for career opportunities, collaborations, and personal development.

Reflection and Actionable Advice:

Platform thinking is all about building a network where resources and people work together to create value. It's not just about what you can do, but about who you can connect with to make it happen.

- Take a moment to reflect on your personal and professional networks. Who's in your ecosystem, and how are you leveraging those relationships? Are you giving as much value as you're receiving?
- Map out your personal "platform." Write down the people, tools, and resources you can tap into to help reach your goals. Include mentors, friends, colleagues, and even online communities.
- Identify one relationship or connection in your platform that you can nurture or strengthen this week. Maybe it's reconnecting with a former colleague, offering to help a friend, or reaching out to a mentor.

By now, it might feel like we took a hard right turn off the roadmap. But hear me out. You've got your roadmap, your toolkit, and your strategies. But life (much like product management) is messy, unpredictable, and constantly throwing you curveballs. That's why it's essential to use **systems thinking**, **frugal innovation**, and **platform thinking** together as you craft your life roadmap. Consider how they all work together:

- **Systems Thinking** helps you see the big picture—so you know how every decision fits into the broader context of your life.

- **Frugal Innovation** keeps you grounded, ensuring you're making the most of your limited resources and staying nimble.
- **Platform Thinking** reminds you that you don't have to go it alone—your success is built on the network of relationships, resources, and opportunities that surround you.

So, as you chart your course, remember life is both a strategic game and a juggling act. You've got to keep the pieces moving, be adaptable when things change, and—most importantly—lean on your network to help you grow. After all, every great roadmap isn't just about where you're going, but how you get there. And with the right mindset, you'll not only reach your destination but have some fun (and maybe even a few laughs) along the way.

Chapter 8
Continuous Improvement Through the Iterative Process

Welcome to the grand finale—or is it? Not quite. Because, as anyone who's been through a few sessions of product development or life lessons can tell you, this is less of a linear progression and more of an ongoing project that's never quite done. Just when you think you've got everything figured out, a new challenge pops up and reminds you: it's time to iterate.

In product management, the idea of continuous improvement or iteration is baked into everything, and the same goes for life. You're never done improving yourself, and that's the beauty of it. But hey, don't panic—this isn't about striving for perfection. It's about learning from your experiences, tweaking your approach, and getting better every step of the way. Let's dive into how you can adopt the Minimum Viable Product (MVP) mindset, embrace failure as a teacher, use data to make smarter choices, and balance it all with some emotional and ethical wisdom.

The Minimum Viable Product (MVP) Mindset

First, let's tackle the MVP mindset—because who doesn't love a good acronym? In product management, an MVP is the simplest version of a product that delivers value to users. You don't roll out the deluxe, all-the-bells-and-whistles version of your app on day one. Nope. You start with the basics, test it, and then improve. The MVP approach lets you gather feedback without going all-in too soon.

Now, what does that look like in life? Think of it like this: you don't need to be the best version of yourself right out of the gate. (Good news, right?) You're allowed to be a work-in-progress. For example, when learning a new skill—like public speaking or finally nailing the perfect lasagna—start with the MVP version. Give yourself permission to be a little rough around the edges. The goal is to launch the first version of yourself in that area, get feedback, and improve over time.

In real time, let's say you want to run a marathon. The MVP version of yourself doesn't need to be running twenty-six miles tomorrow (unless you enjoy collapsing mid-run). Instead, your MVP might be running just one mile without feeling like your lungs are on fire. Over time, you gather feedback—"Huh, maybe skipping warm-ups was a bad idea," or "Turns out, sneakers with arch support do matter"—and you iterate. Each step is an improvement over the last, and before you know it, you're racing past the finish line.

Embrace your MVP stage, whether it's in relationships, skills, or health. Start simple, gather feedback, and make incremental improvements. Life is a series of beta tests—release Version 1.0 of yourself and keep upgrading.

Learning from Failure: Resilience and Adaptability

Now, let's talk about failure—everyone's least favorite F-word but arguably the most important teacher you'll ever have. In product management, failures are not the end of the road—they're just signposts that say, "Hey, maybe try a different route." When a product feature bombs, you don't give up; you regroup, figure out what went wrong, and come back stronger. The same goes for life. Failure isn't a sign to quit; it's a clue that helps you build resilience and adaptability.

Here's the thing: failure is inevitable, but it's how you respond that defines your growth. Failing fast is a core tenet of product management—meaning, fail quickly, learn from it, and adapt before you waste more resources. Imagine if you spent years on a project only to find out it was all wrong—yikes. Wouldn't you rather know sooner and pivot?

In life, the same principle applies. Whether you're learning a new skill, navigating a relationship, or switching careers, setbacks are going to happen. You can either wallow in the failure (and possibly finish an entire pint of ice cream) or you can extract the lessons and use them to improve. The ability to fail fast and bounce back builds resilience, which is like the superpower that keeps you moving forward, no matter how many times you stumble.

Let's take Thomas Edison as an example. When asked about his many failures before inventing the lightbulb, he famously said, "I have not failed. I've just found 10,000 ways that won't work." Now, that's resilience. Life's failures might not be as historic as Edison's, but they're just as valuable in shaping who you are and what you'll accomplish.

Reflection and Actionable Advice:

The MVP mindset is about starting simple and improving over time. You don't need to be perfect out of the gate—just launch, gather feedback, and iterate.

- Think about a project or personal goal that you've been delaying because you want it to be "just right." How could you take an MVP approach and start sooner with a simpler version?
- Choose one goal or project and create an MVP version. What's the minimum you can do to get started and begin gathering feedback? Whether it's launching a blog, trying a new workout routine, or learning a new skill, start small and iterate as you go.
- Set a timeline to review your progress and make improvements. Don't worry about being perfect—focus on continuous improvement over time.

Failure is an inevitable part of growth, but it's how we handle failure that determines whether we stagnate or evolve.

- Reflect on a recent failure or setback. What lessons did you learn from that experience, and how can you apply them to future challenges?
- Identify one failure or mistake from the past month. Write down what you learned from it and how you can use that lesson to improve. For example, if you failed to meet a deadline at work, figure out what went wrong—did you need better time management, or were you overwhelmed?

- Use this failure as a stepping stone. Make one small change this week based on what you've learned, and track the results.

Behavioral Data Analytics: Making Data-Driven Decisions for Continuous Improvement

We have touched on behavioral data analytics already. However, you might still think that data analytics is only for tech nerds with spreadsheets, but hear me out—it's also for those of us navigating life. In product management, behavioral data analytics is all about tracking how users interact with a product and using that data to make smart decisions. You want to know what's working and what's not, so you can fine-tune and make improvements that actually matter.

In life, data doesn't always come in numbers, but it's still there. Are you paying attention to the signals you're getting? Do you feel happier when you get eight hours of sleep versus six? Are you more productive after that morning run, or does it just make you want to nap at your desk? The point is, you can (and should) use the data from your own life to make informed decisions about what's working and what needs tweaking.

How to Track Your Life Data

- **Journaling:** This is your personal dashboard. Track your moods, energy levels, productivity, and overall well-being. Patterns will emerge, and those patterns are your data points.

- **Habit-Tracking Apps:** Use technology to your advantage. Whether it's tracking your fitness, sleep, or productivity, apps can give you insights into your habits and help you identify areas for improvement.
- **Feedback from Others:** Sometimes, we're blind to our own strengths and weaknesses. Seek feedback from friends, mentors, or coworkers. Their insights can serve as valuable data to help you improve.

Example:

Imagine you're trying to improve your productivity at work. You start tracking how different factors—sleep, exercise, meal timing—affect your focus and energy levels. After a few weeks, you notice that your productivity spikes after a healthy breakfast but dips if you skip lunch. Armed with this data, you make a small tweak: you start packing snacks, and voila, you're back on track.

Reflection and Actionable Advice:

Making data-driven decisions doesn't just apply to businesses—it's a valuable tool for personal growth. The data from your own life can help you make smarter choices.

- Think about a habit or routine you'd like to improve. Are you tracking your performance? Are there any data points you could be using to help you make more informed decisions?
- Start a simple tracking system this week. Whether it's journaling your daily habits, using a habit-tracking app, or noting your moods and productivity, gather data on one specific area of your life.

- After a week, review the data. What patterns do you see? Use these insights to make one adjustment in your routine and track the results over the next week.

Emotional and Ethical Design: Balancing Personal Growth with Well-Being and Ethics

So, you've nailed the MVP mindset, embraced failure, and are making data-driven decisions. But here's where things get tricky: how do you grow while keeping your emotional well-being in check? And—let's not forget—how do you ensure your actions align with your ethics?

In product management, emotional and ethical design is about creating products that not only function well but also make users feel good and keep ethical considerations front and center. Think of it as creating experiences that don't just serve a purpose but also feel right and are right. In life, this is about making choices that align with your personal values and support your emotional health.

Emotional Design in Life:

Just like a well-designed product makes users happy, a well-designed life should make you happy. But that doesn't mean chasing short-term pleasure at the expense of long-term growth. It's about creating balance—making decisions that nurture your emotional health while still pushing you toward your goals.

For example, if you're constantly grinding at work but feel miserable, it's time to ask: Is this emotionally sustainable? You might hit your goals, but at what cost? Emotional design in life is about ensuring that the process of growth doesn't come at the expense of your well-being.

Ethical Design in Life:

Ethics come into play when you're deciding not just what to do, but how to do it. Are you treating people with respect? Are you sticking to your values even when it's hard? Ethical design in life means making choices that reflect who you are and what you believe in, whether it's in personal relationships, career decisions, or even how you treat yourself.

Reflection and Actionable Advice:

Growth isn't just about hitting goals—it's about ensuring your emotional well-being and staying true to your ethics along the way.

- Consider a current goal or project. Are you staying true to your values and maintaining your emotional health in the process? Are there any sacrifices you're making that might not be worth it in the long run?
- Take stock of your emotional well-being this week. Are you feeling overwhelmed, stressed, or drained? If so, identify one way you can adjust your routine to prioritize self-care.
- Reflect on an ethical dilemma you've faced recently. Did you handle it in a way that aligns with your values? If not, think about what changes you can make to ensure you're staying true to your principles moving forward.

Life, much like product management, is all about continuous improvement. It's not about nailing perfection—it's about making the tweaks that get you closer to your goals while keeping your emotional and ethical compass intact. Whether it's starting with an MVP version of yourself, learning from failures (because you will fail), using life's data to make better decisions, or balancing growth with emotional well-being, the key is to keep iterating.

The process never ends, and that's a good thing. With each iteration, you're getting a little closer to the best version of yourself—whatever that looks like for you. So keep tweaking, keep learning, and keep growing, because life, like the best products, is always under development.

Chapter 9
Becoming a Data-Driven Product Manager of You

When it comes to managing life, we often rely on gut feelings, general impressions, and a vague sense that things are going "pretty well" or "not so great." But what if you could approach your personal life with the same data-driven precision as a seasoned product manager? Imagine having a personal dashboard with metrics tracking everything from your happiness levels to your workout consistency—suddenly, life starts to look a lot more manageable. In this chapter, we're diving into the importance of data in making informed life decisions, using tools to track your personal metrics, and leveraging these insights to create your best self.

The Importance of Data in Making Informed Life Decisions

In product management, data is the compass guiding every decision. Whether it's deciding which features to prioritize or understanding why users are abandoning your app, data provides the answers. In life, data can be just as transformative. Tracking key aspects of your well-being can reveal patterns you might otherwise miss. Are you happier on days you exercise? Do you spend less time doom-scrolling when you get eight hours of sleep? Data helps take the guesswork out of self-improvement.

Think of this like being your own personal spy, gathering intel on the most important subject of all—yourself. But unlike in a spy movie, where they painstakingly decipher cryptic clues, your data is right there, ready for the taking. The only thing you need is the right set of tools and the willingness to look at the numbers, even when they tell you things you'd rather ignore (like how much time you really spend on social media).

Tools and Techniques for Tracking Life Metrics

Now that you're sold on the importance of data, let's talk about the tools you can use to track your life metrics. Fortunately, you don't need to be a data scientist or spend hours in front of a spreadsheet. Today's technology has made it easier than ever to collect and analyze data about yourself.

Wearables and Apps

If you've got a smartwatch, congratulations—you're already on the data-driven train. These little gadgets do more than just tell time; they track your steps, monitor your heart rate, and even analyze your sleep. They're like having a personal assistant that records everything for you, allowing you to focus on the big picture.

Not a fan of wearables? No problem. There's an app for

pretty much everything. Whether it's a calorie counter, a habit tracker, or a mood journal, you can find digital tools that cater to your specific needs. And fun fact—most all of these apps and digital tools were developed, produced, and are maintained with the help of product managers! Some popular ones include:

- **Fitbit or Apple Health:** Great for tracking physical health metrics, like steps taken, calories burned, and even sleep quality. If you've ever wondered why your productivity tanks after a late night, this app can probably confirm what you already suspect.
- **Mint or YNAB (You Need a Budget):** If your finances need some TLC, these tools can help you track spending, set budgets, and understand your financial habits. Think of them as the finance coaches you didn't know you needed—except they don't judge you for that one time you bought a dozen houseplants during a retail therapy binge.
- **Habitica or HabitBull:** These apps help you track habits and reward you with points for sticking to your goals. Habitica even gamifies your progress, turning your life into a real-life RPG (role-playing game). Imagine leveling up every time you floss—that's motivation!

When it comes to personal metrics, the options are endless. Track your moods with Daylio, measure productivity with RescueTime, or keep tabs on your mental well-being with Moodfit. With so many options, there's no excuse for living life without a personal metrics dashboard.

Of course, you might have concerns over data ethics and personal tracking. So, let's address the elephant in the room.

Data Ethics and Personal Tracking: Navigating the Fine Line

When diving into the world of personal data, it's easy to get caught up in the excitement of tracking and analyzing every facet of your life. But with great data comes great responsibility. Just like in product management, where ethical considerations are crucial when dealing with user data, your personal tracking endeavors should also be guided by principles of data ethics. After all, your personal data can be both a powerful tool and a potential minefield.

Understanding the Ethical Implications of Personal Data

In product management, data ethics often revolves around how user data is collected, stored, and used. Companies have to consider user consent, data privacy, and how their data practices impact users' lives. Although your personal tracking efforts aren't likely to impact anyone but yourself, it's still wise to consider some of these same ethical principles. For instance:

- **Consent and Awareness:** Are you aware of the data you're collecting on yourself and why? It might sound odd, but it's possible to track too much. When you're constantly monitoring every aspect of your life, it can lead to self-imposed surveillance and even burnout. Decide which metrics are genuinely useful, and give yourself "consent" to track those things—then take a break from the rest.

- **Data Privacy:** Even though this is your data, where and how you store it matters. If you're using tracking apps, consider how your data is being stored and shared. Are the apps collecting data for their own use? Are they secure? Remember, just because it's personal doesn't mean it's private, especially when third-party apps are involved.
- **Potential Impact on Well-being:** In product management, companies must consider how their data practices impact users' mental health and well-being. In your own life, you'll want to reflect on whether all this tracking is actually making you happier or just adding stress. If you find yourself obsessing over every step, calorie, or dollar spent, it might be time to scale back. Data should serve you, not the other way around.

Balancing Insight with Privacy

One of the risks of extensive personal tracking is that you can end up overanalyzing. There's a fine line between productive insight and overwhelming yourself with data. Too much information can lead to decision fatigue, making it harder to act on any of it. Remember, the goal is to improve your quality of life, not to turn yourself into a human spreadsheet.

Consider setting boundaries around what data you track and when. For example, you might decide to focus on just one area at a time—like health or finances—rather than trying to optimize every aspect of your life simultaneously. This not only helps maintain your privacy but also keeps you from drowning in data.

Practical Tips for Ethical Data Tracking

- **Limit Data Collection:** Only track the metrics that truly matter to you. If a particular data point isn't serving a purpose, let it go. For instance, you may not need to track every calorie if your goal is simply to eat more mindfully.
- **Regular Data Reviews:** Just as a product manager would regularly review their data practices, make it a habit to assess your personal tracking. Ask yourself if the metrics you're tracking are still relevant and helpful. If not, adjust accordingly.
- **Use Secure Platforms:** If you're using apps to track your data, opt for ones with strong privacy policies. Look for apps that offer data encryption, don't sell your data to third parties, and allow you to download and delete your data if you choose to.
- **Be Mindful of Sharing:** In an era of oversharing, it can be tempting to post all your data-driven achievements online. But remember that once data is shared, it's out there. Be selective about what you post and consider the potential impact on your privacy and well-being.

By approaching personal data with the same ethical considerations a product manager would for their users, you can ensure that your tracking efforts remain both effective and respectful of your privacy. Data is a tool—use it wisely, and remember that some things are better left untracked.

Still not convinced of the magic of wearables and apps? That's okay—you can always go old school!

The Power of Pen and Paper

If you're more analog-inclined, don't underestimate the power of a good old-fashioned journal. Sometimes, manually jotting down your thoughts, activities, and habits can be just as enlightening as using an app. Plus, there's something satisfying about physically writing things down—it feels a bit like setting your intentions in stone. Finally, studies show that we retain information better when we write it! So this old-school method shouldn't be shrugged off.

Whichever method you choose, the goal is the same: to gather data that will help you understand yourself better. Over time, you'll start to notice patterns and correlations. Maybe you're more productive after a morning workout, or perhaps your mood improves on days when you limit screen time. This data becomes part of your roadmap for making informed decisions and tweaking your habits to optimize your life.

Predicting and Improving Personal Outcomes

Data isn't just about looking back; it's also about predicting the future. Just as product managers use analytics to forecast trends, you can use your personal data to anticipate your own outcomes. Did your mood dip after a week of late nights and takeout? Maybe you can predict that following the same pattern this month will yield similar results.

Here's a practical example: imagine you're trying to improve your fitness. After a month of tracking your exercise, you realize you're more likely to hit the gym on Mondays and Fridays, but Tuesdays and Wednesdays are no-shows. Armed with this data, you decide to make Monday and Friday your high-intensity workout days, while saving your gentler activities for mid-week. By adapting based on your trends, you're setting yourself up for success rather than forcing yourself into routines that don't work.

Case Studies: Transforming Lives Through Data-Driven Decisions

Let's look at how data has made a difference in real people's lives. Take Sarah, a young professional who felt perpetually stressed but couldn't figure out why. By tracking her mood, exercise, and sleep, she discovered a clear pattern: her stress levels were higher on days following late-night Netflix binges. So, she made a data-informed choice to set a bedtime alarm. After just a month, Sarah found herself feeling more balanced, energized, and less like she needed a caffeine IV every morning.

Then there's Tom, who felt he wasn't making financial progress. Using Mint, he tracked his spending and realized that his "small" coffee habit was costing him a cool $150 a month. By brewing coffee at home, he redirected those savings to a travel fund and finally took that vacation he'd been putting off. His finances were better, and his caffeine buzz stayed strong.

In each case, data provided the clarity needed to make meaningful changes. Whether you're after better health, financial stability, or simply more joy in your life, leveraging data can set you on the path to transformation.

The beauty of this approach is that it's all about iteration. You try something, track the results, analyze the data, and adjust. It's the classic product management cycle applied to personal growth. Let's go over a few common areas where you can apply this iterative process:

- **Physical Health:** Track metrics like your exercise routine, diet, sleep, and hydration. Use the data to tweak your routine—maybe you discover that a light jog in the morning boosts your mood, or that cutting back on caffeine after noon improves your sleep quality.
- **Mental Well-being:** Record your daily mood and stress levels, and pay attention to what activities or people impact these. If you find that taking breaks throughout the day lowers your stress, you can build more breaks into your schedule.
- **Productivity:** Track how long you spend on different tasks, and compare it with your output. You may discover that deep work sessions in the morning yield better results than multitasking in the afternoon.

Reflection and Actionable Advice:

- **Start Tracking:** Pick a metric that matters to you—whether it's steps, spending, or screen time. Use a tool that makes tracking easy, and commit to gathering data for at least a month.

- **Analyze the Patterns:** Look for trends in your data. Are there correlations between certain behaviors and how you feel? Use this insight to make small adjustments.
- **Set Goals and Iterate:** Just as a product manager would, set goals based on your data and reassess regularly. Celebrate your wins, adjust for setbacks, and remember that data is your friend—not a scary math teacher.
- **Choose Metrics That Matter to You:** Just as a product manager focuses on the KPIs that align with business goals, you should focus on personal metrics that align with your goals. Whether it's fitness, happiness, or productivity, pick metrics that reflect what you value most.
- **Start Small and Scale Up:** Don't overwhelm yourself with tracking too many metrics at once. Start with one or two areas you want to improve and gradually expand as you get more comfortable with data collection.
- **Be Consistent:** Consistency is key when it comes to gathering meaningful data. Set a reminder or establish a routine to log your metrics at the same time each day. The more consistent you are, the clearer your patterns will become.
- **Analyze and Adjust:** Regularly review your data and adjust as needed. Treat your personal development like a product in beta—always refining and improving based on feedback and results.
- **Celebrate Data-Driven Wins:** When you see positive changes based on your data, celebrate them! It could

be something small like treating yourself to a coffee or something big like planning a weekend getaway. Acknowledging these wins will reinforce the habit of using data to drive growth.

Using data to become the product manager of your life isn't about obsessing over every number or graph; it's about gaining insights that help you make more informed choices. With the right tools, techniques, and a little bit of patience, you can leverage data to live a more intentional, fulfilling life. So go ahead—put on that product manager hat and start crunching the numbers. Your optimized, data-driven life awaits!

Chapter 10
Launching the Best Version of You

So, you've gathered the data, set the goals, and tracked the KPIs. Now it's time to unveil the best version of yourself to the world. Just as a product manager carefully plans a product launch, you too can prepare for your big reveal. In this chapter, we're diving into the essentials of building a personal brand, leveraging emotional design, and using platform thinking to collaborate and connect with others.

Think about how companies build anticipation before a product launch. There's the hype, the teasers, the sneak peeks, and finally, the big reveal. Similarly, you've likely been dropping hints of your transformation along the way—those new habits, the mindset shifts, and the goals you've been quietly smashing. Now, it's time to pull back the curtain and show everyone what you've been working on.

But unlike product launches, where perfection is the name of the game, launching the best version of yourself doesn't mean you have to be flawless. Instead, it's about being transparent, authentic, and ready to showcase your journey.

Preparing for the Big Launch

In product management, a launch is more than just a go-live date—it's a culmination of planning, testing, and refining. Launching your personal growth journey is no different. This is where you show off the new you: the goals you've achieved, the habits you've developed, and the insights you've gained.

So, think of it as your own personal launch party. You might not have confetti or a DJ, but there's definitely a sense of celebration. You're showcasing the culmination of your hard work and dedication, not to mention all the data you've analyzed. In other words, it's time to go public with the brand new you.

Things to consider when preparing for the big launch:

- **Define Your Core Message:** Just as a product has a unique selling proposition, you need to define what sets you apart. What are the key qualities, values, or skills that you've developed? What makes you, well, you? Summarize it in a short, impactful statement—think of it as your personal tagline.
- **Share Your Story:** Personal growth is more than just a list of achievements. It's a narrative, complete with ups, downs, and everything in between. Share your journey, including the challenges you've faced and the lessons you've learned. Remember, authenticity resonates more than perfection. And you never know who you will inspire!
- **Gather Your Tools and Resources:** Just like a product launch requires press kits and marketing

materials, your launch requires the right tools. This could mean updating your resume, revamping your LinkedIn profile, or even curating a portfolio of your accomplishments. Ensure that all your platforms reflect the new, evolved you.

Your launch is about building your new personal brand.

Building a Strong Personal Brand Using Narrative and Emotional Design

In the world of product management, a brand isn't just a logo or a catchy slogan; it's a story. It's the sum total of how a product makes people feel and the values it represents. The same applies to you. Building a personal brand is about crafting a narrative that tells people who you are and what you stand for. Your personal brand is how you present yourself to the world—your values, strengths, and unique quirks. It's what makes you memorable.

Imagine your personal brand as a story. Are you the hero who overcame obstacles? The guide who helps others along the way? Define your role, and use emotional design to communicate it. Maybe your brand includes humor, empathy, or an unstoppable drive. Whatever it is, own it and let it guide how you interact with others.

In the digital age, personal branding also includes your online presence. Social media can be a powerful tool for showcasing your journey, but remember to keep it authentic. No one wants to follow a highlight reel—people are drawn to real stories, imperfections, and all.

. . .

Narrative and Emotional Design

Remember, narrative design is all about storytelling, and the best brands know how to tell a great story. Think of yourself as the main character in your own life story. What challenges have you overcome? What values guide your decisions? By framing your journey as a narrative, you make it easier for others to connect with you on a personal level.

Take Apple, for example. They don't just sell tech gadgets; they sell a lifestyle, an ethos of creativity, simplicity, and innovation. Your personal brand should do the same—reflect your core values and present a story that others can resonate with.

While building your story, don't forget emotional design. Think back and remember that emotional design is about creating connections through feelings. How do you want others to feel when they interact with you? Inspired, motivated, maybe even a little in awe? By understanding the emotions you want to evoke, you can align your actions, words, and even your online presence to reflect that.

For instance, if you want to be seen as approachable and supportive, make sure your interactions—whether online or in person—convey warmth and openness. On the other hand, if you aim to be seen as a thought leader, your content might be more focused on sharing insights, providing guidance, and showcasing your expertise.

In product management, emotional design is all about creating a connection with the user. Similarly, in life, your personal brand should connect with people on an emotional level.

Of course, you can't create that emotional connection without platform thinking. So, let's do a quick review.

Platform Thinking: Collaborating and Connecting with Others

Now, perhaps you are beginning to see the puzzle pieces come together. Remember, platform thinking in product management is all about building ecosystems where value is exchanged, like the App Store or Amazon Marketplace. In product management, platforms like social media networks or app ecosystems thrive on user interactions and collaborations. For you, platform thinking is about building networks—relationships that help you and others grow.

Consider your "platform" as the people who support, challenge, and inspire you. Think of mentors, friends, colleagues, and even acquaintances who contribute to your personal and professional journey. Just as a product thrives on partnerships and user engagement, you too can thrive by building meaningful connections.

Leverage your platform by offering value to others. Share your knowledge, offer support, and create opportunities for collaboration. In doing so, you're not just building a network—you're cultivating a community.

Your personal platform can be any combination of your social media profiles, professional networks, and real-world communities. The goal is to create a space where people can interact with you, learn from you, and share ideas. Here's how you can leverage platform thinking in your personal brand:

- **Choose Your Platforms Wisely:** Not all platforms are created equal, and you don't need to be everywhere. Pick the ones that align best with your personal brand. If you're a visual storyteller, Instagram or Pinterest might be your go-to. If you're sharing professional insights, LinkedIn is your playground.
- **Engage with Others:** Platforms thrive on interaction. Comment on other people's posts, share interesting content, and join discussions. Remember, the goal is to build relationships, not just accumulate followers.
- **Collaborate and Co-Create:** Just as platforms grow through partnerships and integrations, your personal brand can grow through collaboration. This could mean guest blogging, joining a podcast, or working on a project with others in your field. When you collaborate, you not only expand your reach but also bring new perspectives to your audience.

Of course, building your platform will benefit from networking. However, networking isn't just about collecting business cards or LinkedIn connections. It's about building genuine relationships that are mutually beneficial. Here's a tip: instead of always thinking about what others can do for you, consider what you can do for them. Offer to help, share resources, or simply lend an ear. When you give without expecting anything in return, you build trust and goodwill that can lead to long-lasting relationships.

Celebrating Success and Planning for Future Growth

Success isn't just about achieving your goals; it's about acknowledging and celebrating every step along the way. In product management, teams celebrate milestones to boost morale and keep the momentum going. Likewise, as you reach new milestones in your personal journey, take the time to celebrate. Whether it's a dinner out, a night with friends, or a well-deserved day off, these celebrations reinforce your hard work and fuel your next steps.

And while you're celebrating, don't forget to plan for future growth. Just as products continue to evolve after launch, your journey doesn't stop here. Take a moment to look back at your progress and envision where you'd like to go next. Set new goals, track new KPIs, and keep iterating.

Reflection and Actionable Advice:

- **Define Your Brand:** What do you want to be known for? Take time to outline the key traits that define your personal brand and consider how to incorporate these into daily interactions.
- **Build Your Platform:** Identify five people who are part of your personal ecosystem, and consider ways to

1. **Prepare for Your Launch Moment**

- Reflect on what you want to achieve in the next chapter of your life. Are you ready to unveil the changes you've worked so hard on? Whether it's a new career move, a lifestyle change, or a fresh approach to relationships, envision your "launch" and how it will look.

- **Actionable Advice:** Start with a plan. Create a roadmap that outlines the steps you need to take to ensure your launch is successful. This could include milestones, a timeline, and even a soft launch to test the waters. Remember, just as product managers prepare for product launches, you should be prepared to iterate based on feedback and results.

2. Strengthen Your Personal Brand with Authenticity

- Take stock of your personal narrative and ask yourself if it genuinely reflects who you are and who you want to become. A strong personal brand is authentic, consistent, and adaptable to change.
- **Actionable Advice:** Regularly review your personal brand. Just as products evolve, so do people. Update your online profiles, network connections, and even your elevator pitch to ensure that they accurately represent your current self. Don't be afraid to highlight your unique story and passions.

3. Cultivate Collaborative Connections

- Building connections isn't just about collecting business cards; it's about fostering meaningful relationships. Take the time to nurture your network and remember that quality beats quantity.

- **Actionable Advice:** Identify a few key individuals in your network who can serve as accountability partners, mentors, or collaborators. Reach out to them regularly, offer support, and be open to opportunities for collaboration. Just as platform thinking encourages product managers to connect users, think about how you can connect people in your life and create value for all parties involved.

4. Embrace a Mindset of Continuous Improvement

- Growth doesn't end at the launch. To truly succeed, you need to keep evolving. This means regularly assessing your progress and being open to learning and adapting.
- **Actionable Advice:** Set up regular intervals to reflect on your personal and professional development. What's working well? What needs adjustment? Create a feedback loop for yourself where you can assess your achievements and identify areas for improvement. This ongoing process will help you stay aligned with your goals and ensure you're always moving forward.

5. Celebrate Success and Plan for the Future

- Finally, take the time to celebrate your successes, big and small. Recognize the effort you've put in and the progress you've made. Celebrations are not just about rewarding yourself but also about reinforcing positive behaviors that drive long-term success.

- **Actionable Advice:** After each significant milestone, take a moment to celebrate—whether that means treating yourself to something special, sharing your success with friends and family, or simply reflecting on your journey. Once the confetti settles, set new goals and start planning your next steps. The journey doesn't stop here; it's just the beginning.

By launching the best version of yourself, strengthening your personal brand, and building a supportive network, you're setting the foundation for a future of continuous growth and success. Remember, you are the product, and life is your roadmap. Enjoy the journey, embrace the challenges, and always be ready to adapt and evolve.

Conclusion: Embracing Life as a Continuous Product Journey

As we wrap up this exploration, it's clear that life is the ultimate product—a constantly evolving, perpetually interesting, and sometimes messy creation. Much like any great product, your life requires continuous growth, adaptation, and a fair bit of maintenance. Throughout this book, we've reimagined product management concepts as tools for self-improvement, taking KPIs, SMART goals, platform thinking, and more, and applying them to the intricate, multifaceted project that is you.

Just as a product manager never stops iterating, learning, and improving, you have the power to continuously enhance your life. Embracing this mindset means you're always a work in progress, and that's something to celebrate! Each new phase of life is a fresh product launch, each challenge is an opportunity for a pivot, and each goal achieved is a milestone on your lifelong roadmap.

You're both the creator and the consumer of your life journey. Unlike products that eventually reach end-of-life, you have the unique privilege of being a product that can perpetually reinvent itself. As you apply these product management principles to your life, remember that you're not just a manager—you're the visionary, the user, and the one who reaps the rewards of your efforts.

Keeping Ethics and Sustainability in Mind

As your life's product manager, it's essential to manage it with ethics and sustainability in mind. Just as successful products consider their impact on the world, the choices you make in your life should ideally reflect not only what's good for you but what's beneficial for those around you. Think about the legacy you want to leave behind and the values you want to uphold.

Sustainable living isn't just about environmental consciousness—it's about creating habits, relationships, and routines that nourish you and the people you care about over the long term. In managing your life product, strive for balance, and remember that your well-being, along with that of your "users" (friends, family, and community), is a crucial part of success.

Final Thoughts and Encouragement: Applying Product Management Principles to Your Life

By embracing life as a product that can be managed, iterated upon, and continuously improved, you're taking charge in a way that aligns with your values and aspirations. It's empowering to see yourself through the lens of product management, where challenges become opportunities, and data-driven decisions lead to growth.

Remember, there's no perfect formula, and no two "products" will look the same. But by equipping yourself with the right tools, frameworks, and a little bit of humor, you're well on your way to crafting a life that's uniquely yours—built with purpose, driven by goals, and open to constant evolution. Embrace the journey, celebrate your wins, and remember: You're the most important product you'll ever manage. Now, go out there and make it great!

Acknowledgements

This book is a reflection of lessons learned from over a decade of professional experience, real-life encounters, and the stories shared by others. Along this journey, countless individuals (products) have inspired me in immeasurable ways.

I am deeply grateful to the many mentors, managers, and leaders who invested their time and energy to shape my skills and exemplify the essence of strong leadership. I owe much to my colleagues in engineering, design, and product management, who taught me what it means to be part of an exceptional product team.

The connection between life and product management has been a topic of many thought-provoking conversations with friends and peers. Each dialogue not only enriched my understanding but also pushed me to become a better storyteller and thinker.

This book has also been profoundly influenced by the insights and work of some of the most respected voices in product management and behavioral sciences: Eric Ries, James Clear, Daniel Kahneman, Angela Duckworth, Nir Eyal, Richard Thaler, and many others. Their groundbreaking ideas helped shape this book into something I am proud to share.

Finally, I want to express my heartfelt gratitude to my TechWalk and Silicon Valley community. Their support has been instrumental in bringing this book to life.

Thank you everyone who has been my partners in this journey directly or indirectly. I know your encouragement will play a vital role in the success of this endeavour.

Rupa Bhagwat, January 2025

Appendix: Templates, Tools, and Exercises for Your Life Management Journey

To help you take action on the concepts covered in this book, this appendix offers templates, tools, and exercises designed to make your self-improvement journey more structured and practical. Use them as a guide, but feel free to adapt them to suit your personal needs.

Additional Resources and Recommended Reading

Here are some resources to deepen your understanding of the concepts covered in this book:

- **"The Lean Startup" by Eric Ries**- A must-read on innovation and continuous improvement.
- **"Atomic Habits" by James Clear**- An in-depth look at how small habits lead to big changes.
- **"Thinking, Fast and Slow" by Daniel Kahneman**- A fascinating dive into how we make decisions.

- **"Grit: The Power of Passion and Perseverance" by Angela Duckworth**- Insights into the importance of resilience.
- **"Hooked: How to Build Habit-Forming Products" by Nir Eyal**- A must-read on creating compelling products (or habits).

Templates and Tools

These templates are here to help you organize your thoughts, set your goals, and stay on track:

Goal-Setting Template (SMART and PACT Goals)

1. **SMART Goal:**What do you want to achieve?
   Now make it:

   - **Specific:**What exactly do you want to accomplish?
   - **Measurable:**How will you know when you've reached your goal?
   - **Achievable:**Is this goal realistic for you?
   - **Relevant:**Why does this goal matter to you?
   - **Time-Bound:**What is your deadline?

2. **PACT Goal:**What do you want to achieve?
   Now make it:

   - **Purposeful:**Does the goal have meaning and long-term purpose for you?

- **Actionable:**Is the goal actionable and controllable? No overplanning!
- **Continuous:**Are the steps you need to take simple and repeatable?
- **Trackable:**NOT measurable—can you say "yes" or "no" to finishing the action steps? Did you do "X" today?

Goal Setting and KPI Template

Purpose: To help you define your goals, set measurable KPIs, and track progress over time.

- **Step 1:** Define Your Goal: What do you want to achieve?
- **Step 2:** Set KPIs: How will you measure success?
- **Step 3:** Timeline: What's your deadline?
- **Step 4:** Action Plan: What steps will you take?

Goal
Key Performance Indicators (KPIs)
Timeline
Action Steps
Example: Improve Health
Exercise 3x per week, 7 hrs sleep
3 months
Join a gym, set workout schedule, track sleep

. . .

Example KPIs:

- **Area:** (e.g., Health, Career, Relationships)
- **KPI:** What specific metric will you track?
- **Target:** What are you aiming for?
- **Progress Tracking:** Record progress at regular intervals (weekly, monthly, etc.).

Personal SWOT Analysis Template

- **Strengths:** What are you naturally good at? What do others admire about you?
- **Weaknesses:** What areas could use improvement? Where do you struggle?
- **Opportunities:** What resources or support systems can you leverage?
- **Threats:** What obstacles stand in your way?

Purpose: To help you identify your strengths, weaknesses, opportunities, and threats in both personal and professional areas.

- **Step 1:** List your strengths. What do you excel at?
- **Step 2:** Identify your weaknesses. What holds you back?
- **Step 3:** Consider your opportunities. What external factors can you leverage?
- **Step 4:** Recognize your threats. What obstacles might you face?

Strengths
Weaknesses
Example: Strong communication
Example: Procrastination

Opportunities
Threats
Example: New job opportunity
Example: Economic uncertainty

EXERCISES

Reflection and Goal Adjustment Exercises

Purpose: To prompt regular reflection on your goals, identify areas for improvement, and adjust as needed.

- **Frequency:** Monthly or quarterly.
- **Exercise Questions:**
    - What goals have I achieved this period?
    - What barriers did I face, and how did I overcome them?
    - Are my goals still aligned with my values and long-term vision?
    - What adjustments do I need to make for continued progress?

Data Tracking Template

Purpose: To assist in tracking personal data for informed decision-making.

- **Step 1:** Define What to Track: Health metrics, productivity, or emotional well-being.
- **Step 2:** Set Frequency: Daily, weekly, or monthly.
- **Step 3:** Analyze Data: What patterns emerge?
- **Step 4:** Make Adjustments: How can you optimize based on your data?

Metric
Frequency
Tracking Method
Observations and Adjustments
Example: Sleep
Daily
Sleep App
Aim for 7-8 hours; adjust evening routine.

Chapter Exercises

ach chapter included tools to help you apply the content. Here are exercises you can use to go deeper:

Chapter 1: The Basics of Product Management Applied to Life

- Identify your "core feature" as a product. What is the most important trait or skill you offer?
- Identify a personal "product" (project or goal) and outline its value proposition.

Chapter 2: Identifying Your Core Values

- Write down your top five core values. Think about how each aligns with the choices you make in daily life.

Chapter 3: Understanding the Market—Life's Challenges and Opportunities

- Conduct a Personal SWOT Analysis using the template. Reflect on what you can do to enhance strengths and mitigate weaknesses.

Chapter 4: Building Your Personal Product Team

- List your personal "advisors," "team members," or support network. Are there gaps? Who could you add to your team?

Chapter 5: Setting Goals and Measuring Success

- Set one SMART and one PACT goal. Track progress for a month and note any adjustments you make along the way.

Chapter 6: Crafting Your Life Roadmap

- Break down your goals into manageable phases. What are your short-term and long-term milestones?

Chapter 7: Continuous Improvement—The Iterative Process of Life

- Reflect on a recent failure. How can you pivot, and what steps can you take to improve?
- Choose an area for improvement and outline an MVP approach to get started.

Chapter 8: Becoming a Data-Driven Product Manager of Your Life

- Identify three personal metrics (KPIs) to track for the next three months. Note any changes and evaluate their impact on your life.
- Track and analyze one habit for a week, then adjust based on the results.

Chapter 9: Launching the Best Version of You

- Craft a personal mission statement. Share it with a friend or mentor and get feedback.
- Outline your personal brand story and reflect on how you present yourself.

Chapter 10: Embracing Life as a Continuous Product Journey

- Set a time to reflect on your progress every quarter. What have you accomplished, and what areas still need attention?
- List three ways to celebrate recent wins, and consider how you'll continue evolving.

By taking these exercises seriously, you'll be well-equipped to handle whatever life throws at you. Keep iterating, stay true to your core values, and never stop building the best version of you. The tools are in your hands, and the journey is yours to enjoy.

References

Chapter 1: The Basics of Product Management Applied to Life

1. **Eyal, N., & Hoover, R.**(2014). Hooked: How to Build Habit-Forming Products. Penguin Random House.

A comprehensive guide on creating habit-forming products by leveraging psychological triggers and behavior design.

2. **Kahneman, D.**(2011). Thinking, Fast and Slow. Farrar, Straus and Giroux.

An influential book on behavioral economics, cognitive biases, and decision-making processes.

3. **Thaler, R. H., & Sunstein, C. R.**(2021). Nudge: The Final Edition. Yale University Press.

This edition expands on the original ideas of nudging to encourage better decision-making in both personal and professional contexts.

4. **Cagan, M., & Jones, C.**(2017). INSPIRED: How to Create Products Customers Love. SVPG Press.

A product management classic on building successful products through customer-centric strategies and life-cycle management.

5. **Maurya, A.**(2016). Scaling Lean: Mastering the Key Metrics for Startup Growth. Penguin Random House.

Provides actionable insights on using metrics to scale products during the introduction phase, relevant to both personal and professional growth.

6. **Blank, S., & Dorf, B.**(2020). The Startup Owner's Manual: The Step-By-Step Guide for Building a Great Company. Wiley.

A comprehensive guide on scaling startups, with parallels for personal development during the growth phase.

7. **Croll, A., & Yoskovitz, B.**(2013). Lean Analytics: Use Data to Build a Better Startup Faster. O'Reilly Media.

Discusses the maturity phase of product management, focusing on how data and analytics support long-term success.

8. **Gans, J. S.**(2016). The Disruption Dilemma. The MIT Press.

Examines how industries and individuals face disruption, with insights into how to pivot and reinvent during the decline phase.

Chapter 2: Identifying Your Core Values - The Foundation of Your Product

1. **Brown, B.**(2018). Dare to Lead: Brave Work. Tough Conversations. Whole Hearts. Random House.

Discusses the importance of identifying and leading with core values in both life and business.

2. **Thaler, R. H., & Sunstein, C. R.**(2021). Nudge: The Final Edition. Yale University Press.

Explores how behavioral economics and decision science influence personal goal-setting and ethics.

3. **Goleman, D., Boyatzis, R., & McKee, A.**(2017). Primal Leadership: Unleashing the Power of Emotional Intelligence. Harvard Business Review Press.

Focuses on ethics in leadership and emotional intelligence in personal and professional settings.

4. **Brown, B.**(2015). Rising Strong: How the Ability to Reset Transforms the Way We Live, Love, Parent, and Lead. Random House.

Discusses the role of resilience as a core feature in navigating life's challenges.

5. **Grant, A.**(2021). Think Again: The Power of Knowing What You Don't Know. Viking.

Explores the value of rethinking and learning from mistakes, relevant to building resilience.

Chapter 3: Understanding the Market: Life's Challenges and Opportunities

1. **Rothaermel, F. T.**(2021). Strategic Management: Concepts and Cases. McGraw-Hill Education.

A comprehensive resource on SWOT analysis and strategic management in both corporate and personal contexts.

2. **Meadows, D. H., & Wright, D.**(2015). Thinking in Systems: A Primer. Chelsea Green Publishing.

Provides an introduction to systems thinking and how it can be applied to life's complex systems.

3. **Hammersley, M., & Atkinson, P.**(2019). Ethnography: Principles in Practice (4th ed.). Routledge.

A guide on using ethnographic methods to understand

cultures and environments, with applications in personal and professional life.

4. **Bocken, N. M. P., Short, S. W., Rana, P., & Evans, S.**(2018). "A Literature and Practice Review to Develop Sustainable Business Model Archetypes." Journal of Cleaner Production, 65, 42-56.

A review of sustainable business models that offers insights into applying sustainability principles to personal decision-making.

5. **Sinek, S.**(2019). The Infinite Game. Portfolio.

Discusses the importance of creating a personal vision that focuses on long-term, sustainable success rather than short-term wins.

Chapter 4: Building Your Personal Product Team

1. **Feld, B.**(2020). The Startup Community Way: Evolving an Entrepreneurial Ecosystem. Wiley.

Examines how building strong, diverse teams and ecosystems is essential for both businesses and individuals.

2. **Johnson, W. B., & Ridley, C. R.**(2018). The Elements of Mentoring (3rd ed.). Macmillan.

A guide to effective mentoring relationships, applicable to career transitions and personal growth.

3. **Norman, D. A., & Stappers, P. J.**(2015). DesignX: Complex Sociotechnical Systems. She Ji: The Journal of Design, Economics, and Innovation.

Explores inclusive design and creating environments that foster diverse perspectives.

4. **Gottschall, J.**(2015). The Storytelling Animal: How Stories Make Us Human. Mariner Books.

Discusses the power of narrative design in crafting personal and professional stories that resonate.

5. **Norman, D. A.**(2021). The Design of Everyday Things: Revised and Expanded Edition. Basic Books.

Explores emotional design and how emotional connections are built through products, relationships, and experiences.

6. **Rogers, E. M.**(2003). Diffusion of Innovations (5th ed.). Free Press.

A foundational text on the product adoption curve and how innovations spread, with parallels to personal relationships.

7. **Moore, G. A.**(2014). Crossing the Chasm: Marketing and Selling High-Tech Products to Mainstream Customers (3rd ed.). Harper Business.

Explores how innovations move from early adopters to the mainstream, with insights applicable to building personal and professional networks.

Chapter 5: The Wonderful World of KPIs

1. **McKeown, G.**(2021). Effortless: Make It Easier to Do What Matters Most. Currency.

A guide to setting personal goals and KPIs in a way that reduces stress and maximizes efficiency.

Chapter 6: A Practical Guide to Goal Setting

1. **Clear, J.**(2018). Atomic Habits: An Easy & Proven Way to Build Good Habits & Break Bad Ones. Avery.

A practical guide to setting SMART goals and building habits through incremental improvements.

2. **Milkman, K. L.**(2021). How to Change: The Science of

Getting from Where You Are to Where You Want to Be. Portfolio.

Discusses decision science and how precommitment strategies can help you achieve your personal and professional goals.

3. **Covey, S. R.**(2020). The 7 Habits of Highly Effective People: 30th Anniversary Edition. Simon & Schuster.

Explores the Eisenhower Matrix and how prioritizing tasks can lead to more effective time management and goal achievement.

4. **American Society of Training and Development (ASTD).**(2014). The Importance of Accountability in Achieving Goals. Research Study.

A study showing that individuals with accountability partners are significantly more likely to achieve their goals.

5. **Harvard Business Review.**(2017). How Accountability Fuels Collaboration and Team Performance. Harvard Business Review.

An article that discusses the role of accountability in boosting individual and team performance.

6. **Dominican University of California.**(2018). The Power of Accountability: Research on Goal Setting. Study by Dr. Gail Matthews.

A study showing that writing down goals and sharing them with an accountability partner significantly improves goal achievement.

7. **Zichermann, G., & Linder, J.**(2015). The Gamification Revolution: How Leaders Leverage Game Mechanics to Crush the Competition. McGraw-Hill Education.

A practical guide to using gamification to boost engagement, applicable in both product management and personal goal-setting.

8. **Hubbard, D. W.**(2020). How to Measure Anything: Finding the Value of Intangibles in Business (3rd ed.). Wiley.

Discusses behavioral data analytics and how it can be used to track progress and optimize personal development.

9. **Amabile, T. M., & Kramer, S. J.**(2011). The Progress Principle: Using Small Wins to Ignite Joy, Engagement, and Creativity at Work. Harvard Business Review Press.

A book that discusses the power of recognizing small wins to maintain motivation and enhance creativity in the workplace.

10. **Anseel, F., et al.**(2018). How Feedback Boosts Motivation: Exploring the Role of Goal Progress. Organizational Behavior and Human Decision Processes, 144, 1-14.

This study explores how feedback and recognizing goal progress can increase employee motivation.

11. **Allen, D. G., et al.**(2019). How Recognition Impacts Employee Retention: A Meta-Analysis. Journal of Applied Psychology, 104(5), 629-653.

A comprehensive study showing how employee recognition improves retention, job satisfaction, and mental well-being.

12. **Zenger, J.**(2018). "The Power of Recognition in the Workplace." Forbes.

This article discusses how recognition and celebration of milestones in the workplace improve collaboration and team motivation.

Chapter 7: Crafting Your Life Roadmap – Strategies for Success

1. **Meadows, D. H., & Wright, D.**(2015). Thinking in Systems: A Primer. Chelsea Green Publishing.

A comprehensive guide on systems thinking, offering practical examples of how interconnectedness and feedback loops influence decision-making and long-term success.

2. **Govindarajan, V., & Trimble, C.**(2012). Reverse Innovation: Create Far From Home, Win Everywhere. Harvard Business Review Press.

This book dives into frugal innovation and how resource-limited environments can inspire innovative solutions that apply globally.

3. **Gawer, A.**(2014). Platform Leadership: How Intel, Microsoft, and Cisco Drive Industry Innovation. Harvard Business Review Press.

A key resource on platform thinking in product management, detailing how platforms can leverage networks for growth and long-term success.

4. **Brown, T.**(2019). Change by Design: How Design Thinking Transforms Organizations and Inspires Innovation. HarperBusiness.

Explores how design thinking and platform thinking can transform products and personal growth by tapping into creativity and collaboration.

5. **Pisano, G. P.**(2019). Creative Construction: The DNA of Sustained Innovation. PublicAffairs.

This book emphasizes systems thinking in organizations and how individuals can apply these principles to personal growth, particularly in terms of anticipating long-term impacts.

Chapter 8: Continuous Improvement—The Iterative Process of Life

1. **Ries, E.**(2011). The Lean Startup: How Today's Entrepreneurs Use Continuous Innovation to Create Radically Successful Businesses. Crown Publishing.

A foundational text on the Minimum Viable Product (MVP) mindset, emphasizing continuous improvement and how iteration is essential to success.

2. **Grant, A.**(2021). Think Again: The Power of Knowing What You Don't Know. Viking.

This book emphasizes the importance of learning from failure, building resilience, and the adaptability required for continuous improvement in both work and life.

3. **Milkman, K. L.**(2021). How to Change: The Science of Getting from Where You Are to Where You Want to Be. Portfolio.

Explores how behavioral data and decision science can drive continuous improvement in personal development, drawing on the latest psychological research.

4. **Norman, D. A.**(2021). The Design of Everyday Things: Revised and Expanded Edition. Basic Books.

Discusses emotional and ethical design principles in product development, offering insights on how to balance functionality with emotional well-being.

5. **Dweck, C. S.**(2016). Mindset: The New Psychology of Success. Ballantine Books.

Covers the importance of a growth mindset in continuous improvement, learning from setbacks, and balancing personal growth with emotional resilience.

Chapter 9: Becoming a Data-Driven Product Manager of Your Life

1. **Marr, B.**(2020). Data Strategy: How to Profit from a World of Big Data, Analytics and the Internet of Things. Kogan Page. A guide to understanding the value of data and how it can be applied to decision-making in both business and personal contexts.

2. **McAfee, A., & Brynjolfsson, E.**(2017). Machine, Platform, Crowd: Harnessing Our Digital Future. W. W. Norton & Company. An exploration of how data-driven decisions are transforming industries and personal lives by leveraging digital tools and platforms.

3. **Patel, N.**(2019). "The Power of Data-Driven Decision-Making in Personal Life." Forbes. An article on the impact of data-driven decision-making, offering examples of how individuals can apply analytics to improve various aspects of their lives.

4. **Davenport, T. H., & Kim, J.**(2013). Keeping Up with the Quants: Your Guide to Understanding and Using Analytics. Harvard Business Review Press. This book provides insight into how anyone, not just analysts, can use data to make more informed decisions.

5. **Milkman, K. L.**(2021). How to Change: The Science of Getting from Where You Are to Where You Want to Be. Portfolio. A deep dive into behavioral data and how tracking habits and decisions can lead to meaningful change.

Chapter 10: Launching the Best Version of You

1. **Gallo, C.**(2019). The Storyteller's Secret: From TED Speakers to Business Legends, Why Some Ideas Catch On and Others Don't. St. Martin's Press. A look at how storytelling and personal branding can be transformative tools for connecting with others and achieving success.

2. **Goldman, J.**(2017). The Power of Connection: How To Become a Master Communicator In Your Personal and Professional Life. New Harbinger Publications. Explores how emotional design and platform thinking can be used to build strong, authentic connections.

3. **Kleon, A.**(2014). Show Your Work!: 10 Ways to Share Your Creativity and Get Discovered. Workman Publishing Company. A practical guide on personal branding and the importance of sharing your journey to connect with others.

4. **Brown, T.**(2009). Change by Design: How Design Thinking Transforms Organizations and Inspires Innovation. HarperBusiness. Discusses the importance of narrative and emotional design, particularly in creating memorable and impactful personal brands.

5. **Grant, A.**(2021). Think Again: The Power of Knowing What You Don't Know. Viking. Offers insights on continuous learning, adaptation, and the value of reflecting on and re-evaluating personal growth for future success.

www.ingramcontent.com/pod-product-compliance
Lightning Source LLC
LaVergne TN
LVHW010100170826
845678LV00012B/2188

* 9 7 9 8 8 9 6 9 1 0 4 5 9 *